CLASSIC GUNS OF THE WORLD SERIES

THE LUGER
P.08 VOL. 2
THIRD REICH AND POST-WWII MODELS

THE LUGER P.08 VOL. 2

THIRD REICH AND POST-WWII MODELS

LUC GUILLOU

& GEORGES MACHTELINKX

CLASSIC GUNS OF THE WORLD SERIES

LUGER P.08

MARKINGS

VARIANTS

AMMUNITION

ACCESSORIES

MILITARY

4880 Lower Valley Road   Atglen, PA 19310

Originally published as *Le Luger: Un pistolet de légende, deuxième partie* by Regi'Arm, Paris © 2001 Regi'Arm
Translated from the French by Julia and Frédéric Finel

Library of Congress Control Number: 2018959814

Cover design by Justin Watkinson
Type set in Helvetica Neue LT Pro/Times New Roman

ISBN: 978-0-7643-6188-3
Printed in China

Published by Schiffer Publishing, Ltd.
4880 Lower Valley Road
Atglen, PA 19310
Phone: (610) 593-1777; Fax: (610) 593-2002
E-mail: Info@schifferbooks.com
Web: www.schifferbooks.com

For our complete selection of fine books on this and related subjects, please visit our website at www.schifferbooks.com.
You may also write for a free catalog.

Schiffer Publishing's titles are available at special discounts for bulk purchases for sales promotions or premiums. Special editions, including personalized covers, corporate imprints, and excerpts, can be created in large quantities for special needs.
For more information, contact the publisher.

We are always looking for people to write books on new and related subjects. If you have an idea for a book, please contact us at proposals@schifferbooks.com.

CONTENTS

Several P.08s made under French control: *top*, on a Parachutist beret and an amateur-made holster, a P.08 bearing the number 3330. This unstamped example with a toggle marked "S/42" and a chamber with the year 41 is very uncharacteristic. It was possibly assembled in a French arsenal from spare parts retrieved before the destruction of the Mauser factory. A French-produced tool is to the right of the weapon. Another P.08 made under French control with a chamber dated 42. This example bears the number 2976 and the "Eagle/N" stamp. Example with an undated chamber, serial number 1979, preceded by the "Eagle/N" stamp.

FOREWORD

The Luger pistol was originally designed by the DWM company of Berlin, where mass production began in 1900. The version of the Luger adopted by the German army in 1908, the P.08, was also made by the royal arsenal at Erfurt starting in 1911.

At the armistice of 1918, the Erfurt facilities were dismantled and DWM somehow continued to assemble the P.08 for commercial use. In parallel, Simson & Co. of Suhl made the P.08 in small quantities for the Reichswehr as part of the machine tools that had been retrieved from the Erfurt arsenal.

The part of the Luger story that took place from 1900 to the emergence of the Third Reich was presented in the first volume. This second volume covers the following:

- the Luger made in Germany under the Third Reich by the Mauser and Krieghoff factories

- the Luger pistols used, assembled, or made following the Second World War

- several models in the Luger family: Swiss, "American Eagle," Dutch, Portuguese

- accessories relating to the different types of Luger: holsters, magazines, tools, conversions, manuals, etc.

CHAPTER 1

THE MAUSER LUGERS

The Mauser factory sports team leaving the company stadium, where the logos of Mauser and DWM can be seen under the gate. Note the similarity of the DWM logo design to that of the Mauser logo.

Blank Toggle P.08

COMMERCIAL MAKES

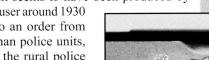

We have grouped all Luger pistols destined for users other than the German army under this name; these include

- private individuals and private associations

- foreign armies or police forces

- German administrative bodies (police, customs, etc.)

THE BLANK TOGGLE P.08

A first variant seems to have been produced by BKIW or Mauser around 1930 to respond to an order from certain German police units, in particular the rural police (Landjägerei). This is the standard-type P.08, in 9 mm Para caliber, or more rarely 7.65 mm Parabellum, which differ from the usual models due to the presence of a toggle

without any marking.[1] The majority of these weapons bear a serial number from one to four figures followed by one letter: "s," "t," or "u."

Due to the fact that these P.08 were used by the police, they often had supplementary safety devices such as Schywie and Walther.[2]

Some of these pistols bear the unit markings of the police units on the grip.[3]

In addition to the type "vertical Crown N" standard commercial test stamps, these weapons have very typical stamps (Eagle/H and Eagle / WaA 66) on the right side of the slide.

WaA 66 stamped on the left side of this weapon.

The Schlewsig rural police marking (Landjägerei Schleswig weapon number 19)

At the end of the 1930s, DWM became part of a vast complex that grouped together other German weapons factories and took the name of "BKIW" (Berlin-Karlsruher Industrie-Werken A.G.). The Mauser factories were also part of this group.

From 1930 onward, BKIW decided that the DWM site should specialize in manufacturing ammunition, and transferred the P.08 assembly lines to the Mauser factories at Oberndorf.

MILITARY MAKES

Between 1930 and 1942, Mauser produced the P.08 for commercial use and for the German army. The commercial production made up the majority of Luger output up to 1934. After the National Socialists gained power in 1933, and the start of a policy of intensive rearmament the following year, the manufacture of the P.08 for the German army increased steadily.

Starting in 1936, the majority of the P.08s made by Mauser were destined for the armed forces (Wehrmacht). From this period, the sales of "commercial" weapons diminished compared to those for military use.

At Mauser the mass production of the P.08 ended during 1942. This firm limited itself to the manufacture of the P.38 and HSc pistols until the end of the war.

1. This variant often goes under the name of "Blank Toggle" or "Sneak." However, these names are gradually being abandoned by collectors in favor of "Model 29," which indicates the probable date of production of these weapons. This name is not necessarily accurate, since, first, this is not a "model" in the strictest sense, and, second, there is still uncertainty as to the exact date of manufacture of this variant. In order to avoid any confusion, this variant will be referred to as "Blank Toggle" in this edition.
2. These are presented in volume 1.
3. An Interior Ministry directive of February 1937 stipulated the end of the police unit markings.

Scene on the Eastern Front, probably reconstructed by the German propaganda services, showing the arrest of a group of partisans by the police. The majority of the men in the group are armed with the P.08. *ECPA*

Small "Mauser Banner"

Large "Mauser Banner"

Template used to apply the Mauser Banner logo on the P.08 toggles

Mauser inspection stamp commonly seen on commercial weapons. This marking represents the "M" and "R" of Mauser intertwined.

MAUSER PRODUCTIONS WITH DWM-MARKED TOGGLE

In addition to the use of the blank toggles, the Mauser factories continued to use toggles marked with the DWM logo for several years, both for the German market and for export. This use of DWM-marked toggles by Mauser was probably justified by the desire to use up spare parts inherited from the initial manufacturer, as well as the desire not to disrupt the clients' habits too much during the early days of the manufacture of the Luger at Oberndorf.

Some of these pistols were used by the army and the navy at Weimar, and others were delivered to Finland.[4] These P.08s can have a commercial- or military-type numbering; they have type "vertical Crown N"[5] commercial test stamps, and many were exported to the United States. The models delivered to the Stoeger firm have the American eagle on the toggle and the company name of the importer on the right side of the slide (see section on the "American Eagle" Luger).

MAUSER PRODUCTIONS WITH "MAUSER BANNER"–MARKED TOGGLE

At the beginning of the century, Mauser patented the design of a commercial logo called "Mauser Banner,"[6] which was put on various commercial productions (in particular on certain 7.65 mm or 6.35 mm Browning pocket pistols, but also on some hunting rifles and even on military weapons such as the TG 18 antitank rifle or certain Mauser 98s).

On a date that has still not been determined, the Luger toggles produced by Mauser for the commercial circuit were struck with this logo, of which there are two variants:

- The first, of a small size, was initially used during a brief period (particularly on a batch delivered to Sweden, on the Luger for the Garde Nationale Republicaine du Portugal contract, and on certain commercial weapons delivered to Switzerland).

- The second, larger variant was used on commercial versions until the production of the P.08 was stopped at Oberndorf.

Among the buyers of these P.08 "Mauser Banner" were the following:

- individual private buyers in Germany or abroad

- The German police,[7] who ordered them in large quantities. The police weapons are easily identifiable by the presence of police acceptance stamps (Eagle/C or Eagle/L in general) and by the addition of a Schywie safety on the trigger side plate.

OPPOSITE PAGE: Several "commercial" Lugers made by Mauser, *from top to bottom*: with 20 cm barrel in 9 mm caliber (no. 3052) made for Persia, with 20 cm barrel in 9 mm caliber (no. 3484v), for Siam. With 10 cm barrel in 9 mm caliber (no. 2893), delivered to Persia, with 12 cm barrel in 7.65 mm caliber (no. 1935v), for the Republican National Guard of Portugal (GNR). Safety lock at the rear of the grip, chamber marked "GNR," safety zone and extractor marked "Seguranca" and "Carregada," test stamp: "U" with double crown in a horizontal position.
With 12 cm barrel in 7.65 mm caliber (no. 1894v) for commercial sale in Switzerland, safety lock at the rear of the grip, with bolt marked DWM (no. 411v), delivered to the American importer Stoeger ("American Eagle" marking on the chamber, safety zones and extractor marked "Safe" and "Loaded," test stamp (crowned "N"), with 12 cm barrel in 7.65 mm caliber (no. 598v) for commercial sale in Switzerland. Safety lock at the rear of the grip, toggle with small Mauser banner, chamber marked with the Swiss cross surrounded by rays (test stamp: "U" with double crown in vertical position). Among the accessories, note the following (*from top to bottom*): a magazine with a shiny nickel finish (or perhaps chromed?) with an aluminum base, of the most frequently seen type on commercial Mauser productions, a steel rod with cylindrical handle used as a container for lubricant, a blued magazine with wooden bottom, probably made or reconditioned by an arsenal in Portugal, a disassembly tool, a pouch for two spare magazines of the type accompanying the long Parabellums delivered to Persia.

- some foreign weapons: Turkey, the Netherlands, Portugal, Siam, and Persia

All Luger pistols made by Mauser are fitted with a short, P.08-type frame.[8] These weapons could be chambered in 9 mm caliber (the barrel generally was 10 cm in length) or in 7.65 mm Para (in this case, with barrels of 10 cm or more often 12 cm). Some variants were supplied with a handle safety lever.[9]

---

4. See volume 1.
5. The two types of stamp "crowned N" are covered in volume 1.
6. In the 2000 edition of his work *Die Pistole 08*, historian Joachim Görtz points out that the expression "Mauser Tonne" should be used rather than "Mauser Banner." However, the latter has now been used among collectors for a number of years, so it will be used here.
7. From 1936 onward, the different police forces existing in Germany were grouped together into a single organization: the commander of the Reich Main Security Office (RHSA) was placed under the authority of Reichsführer-SS Heinrich Himmler.

Some commercial P.08s have their caliber mentioned on the barrel, as seen here: "Kal. 7,65" on a specimen sold in Sweden.

"Eagle / L" stamped by the police for the reception of the weapon

Another variant of a police reception stamp "Eagle/C"

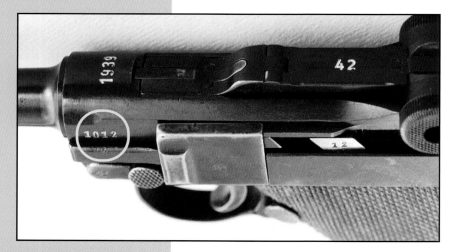

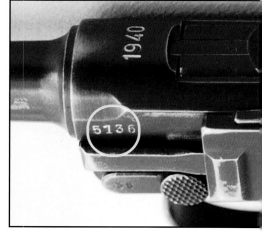

Example of a Mauser commercial test stamp ("U" double crowned, which could be stamped either in a vertical or horizontal position) on the left side of the slide and on the bolt head on these commercial P.08s of 1939. This example has the number 5313W; the small parts were still annealed in yellow, and the grips were in checkered walnut.

Police P.08 No. 5136v. The new commercial stamp of the Reich "Eagle/N" is clearly visible above the number of the weapon and on the left side of the bolt head. Note also the Schywie safety positioned above the trigger side plate. On this example the small parts are blued.

In certain cases, the caliber is mentioned on the barrel ("Kal. 9 mm" or "Kal. 7.65").

The proof stamps are those of the Mauser testing stand: a letter "U" topped by a crown, stamped on the left side of the slide and bolt head and on the front of the front sight mount. From 1940, the Mauser test stamp ("U" with double crown) was abandoned in favor of a new commercial test stamp adopted by the Third Reich: an eagle with outstretched wings topped with a letter *N*.

From the end of 1941, the marking "P.08" appeared on the left side of some frames.

The numbering can be either of a commercial or military type.[10] The serial number is most often followed by the letters "u," "v," "w," "x," or "y."

The chamber can

- have no markings

- have a date marking of two or four figures (in particular on the police P.08)

- have a specific logo marking relevant to certain contracts (initials GNR on the Luger delivered to the Portuguese Republican National Guard, the lion of Persia, the Swiss cross in a sun on some examples exported to Switzerland, or specific markings on the chamber of some Turkish Lugers)

8. With the exception of certain Lugers exported to Switzerland for commercial sale that can be found with a long Mauser-made frame (examples 598v, 1894v, and 3731v are identifiable with this particularity). See the presentation of both types of frame in volume 1, page 61.
9. The Mauser-made variant with safety lock is sometimes called "model 06 / 34" by collectors. This is not an official name.
10. See the definition of these terms in volume 1.

Commercial P.08 No. 8571w, bearing the year of the chamber in two figures: "42" indicating the weapon was made in 1942. Note the marking "P.08" stamped on the left side of the frame, above the grips. Even though this example was made in 1942, it has wooden grips.

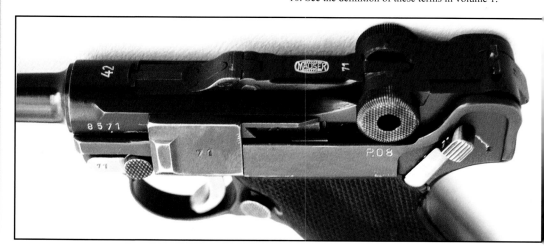

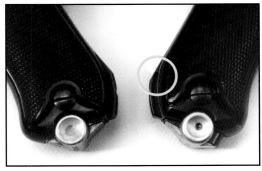

Left: normal back grip; right, grip back with reinforcement called "Mauser Backe."

On the P.08 the stock lug has a small orifice that is not found on the frames made by other manufacturers. This small blind hole was probably used to maintain the part during machining or finishing procedures.

- have markings in the national language on certain contracts (Iranian, Turkish, Portuguese) on the safety and extractor zone

Some of these P.08s had a 20 cm barrel with an adjustable front sight (without micrometric adjustment), with gradations up to a distance of 800 meters. These 9 mm caliber pistols, which took up the shape of the long P.08 made for the imperial German army at the end of the former conflict, were essentially made for Persia and Siam.

The Luger delivered by Mauser to Portugal and the versions delivered to Switzerland for commercial sale are presented in the third part of this edition.

Small deliveries of Luger were sent by Mauser to various countries (Lithuania, Sweden, etc.). These weapons appear not to have had any typical markings. We will limit ourselves therefore in this chapter to present three clearly identifiable variants corresponding to the Turkish, Persian, and Siamese contracts:

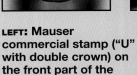

LEFT: Mauser commercial stamp ("U" with double crown) on the front part of the front sight mount

RIGHT: commercial stamp (Eagle/N) in the same position

For some of his official visits, Adolf Hitler traveled in a powerful armored G4-type Mercedes, where Parabellum (probably commercial models) and spare magazines could be hidden in the backs of the seats so passengers and their bodyguards could defend themselves in case of ambush. *Mercedes-Benz Museum Stuttgart*

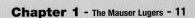

TURKISH CONTRACT

A thousand P.08s were delivered by Mauser to various Turkish state organizations, with the police receiving the major part. Since very few of these weapons have come out of Turkey, their characteristics are only just starting to be known, thanks to the research led by British collector Geoffrey Sturgess.

Three distinct series of Turkish Luger have been identified.[11]

Weapons destined for the security police

Several years before the Second World War (probably around 1936), Mauser delivered 750 type P.08 pistols to the Turkish police, recognizable by their particular markings:

- small Mauser commercial logo on the toggle

In a setting that evokes the first years of the Third Reich, four P.08 commercial Mausers, *from top to bottom*: serial number 5313v, manufactured in 1939, placed on an Akah commercial holster of superb quality; serial number 8571w, manufactured in 1942; serial number 3629v, manufactured in 1936; and serial number 7629w, made for Sweden, placed on a Swedish holster (this example is in 7.65 mm Para caliber, while the three others are in 9 mm). This photo also features holsters and a German prewar box of ammunition made by Gustav Genschow.

numbering is of the military type. The few examples identified have serial numbers without a suffix letter

Turkish P.08 seen from above: small banner toggle and "TC" marking on the chamber. *Albert Beliard*

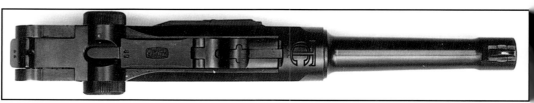

- markings in Turkish on the extractor and the safety zone ("Ates" and "Emniyet," respectively)

- the initials "T" and "C" intertwined on the chamber, signifying Turkiye Cümhüriyeti (Turkish Republic)

- "Emniyet Isleri Umum Müdürlügü" (Security Police) on the right side of the slide. Even though the slide marking is the commercial type, these weapons have the "U" with double-crown commercial stamp on the left side of the slide, and German army inspection stamps (Eagle/63) on the slide, front sight mount, and bolt head. Their

Weapons destined for army officers

Another batch of P.08-type commercial pistols, estimated to be around 250, were destined for officers of the Turkish army.[12] The numbers of these pistols are followed by the letter "v," which places them in the same production group as most other Mauser commercial Lugers. These pistols have the Mauser logo on the toggle, with markings on the extractor and the safety in German. Author Jan Still mentions that known examples have Mauser military-type "Eagle/63" inspection stamps. The chamber is dated 1936. The marking "Subaylara Mahsustur" appears on the right side of the slide; this can be translated as "destined for officers."

"Subaylara Mahsustur" marking on the slide of the version reserved for army officers

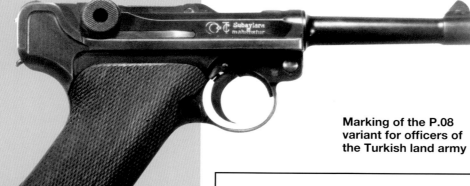

Marking of the P.08 variant for officers of the Turkish land army

11. Provided of course that the examples mentioned are authentic!
12. Currently it is not known if these weapons were directly delivered to the army or if they were bought by the officers personally via the intermediary of a purchasing department.

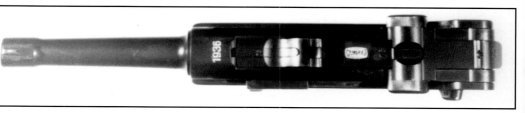

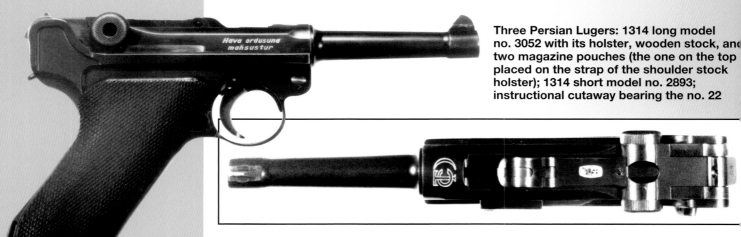

Three Persian Lugers: 1314 long model no. 3052 with its holster, wooden stock, and two magazine pouches (the one on the top placed on the strap of the shoulder stock holster); 1314 short model no. 2893; instructional cutaway bearing the no. 22

Luger destined for the Turkish air force

Persian arms stamped on the chamber of Mauser-made Luger

Marking on the slide of a long Parabellum. Note the stamp of the Persian inspector (in the shape of a crown) who paid Oberndorf for the pistols destined for its country.

Marking on the slide of a 1314 Parabellum short model

Weapons destined for the air force

A later version of the commercial P.08 seems to have been delivered to the Turkish air force. These were onboard weapons, making up part of the usual equipment of fighter planes delivered by Germany to Turkey. These weapons had specific markings, however:

- the initials "T" and "C" on the chamber, followed by a crescent pointing toward the left

- markings on the extractor and the safety zone in Turkish ("Ates" *and* Emniyet")

- the marking "Hava ordusuna mahsustur" ("for the use of the air force") on the right side of the slide

The only example to have been examined by collectors has the number 9014v.

PERSIAN CONTRACT

The contract, agreed between Persia and Mauser in 1936, seems to have concerned 3,000 P.08s, 2,000 of which were the standard type with 10 cm[13] barrel, and 1,000 long type with 20 cm[14] barrel. These weapons were referred to as "model 1314"[15] by the Iranians and have the arms of Iran on the chamber and are marked exclusively in Farsi:

- The toggle has "Mauser Production" in Farsi.

- The marking "loaded" on the left side of the extractor and "safety" on the left side of the frame are also in Farsi.

- "Parabellum long 1314 model" also appears in Farsi on the right side of the slide on models with 20 cm barrel, and "Parabellum short 1314 model" on 10 cm barrel models.

13. Probably numbered from 1 to 2,000. The first fifty example seem to have been used to make instructional cutaways.
14. Numbered from 3,000 (or possibly 3,001) to 4,000 (c 3,999)
15. The year 1314 in the Muslim calendar corresponds to th year 1936 in the Christian calendar.

Marking on a Persian extractor

Marking on a Persian safety

Two examples of Luger made by Mauser for Persia and a long 1314 model and a short version

Example of the serial number marking on a Persian Parabellum. The Mauser commercial test stamp can be seen in front of the number and a small sign resembling a letter "b."

Sight of a long Persian Parabellum, marked in Farsi figures

Marking on the rear of a long Siamese Luger

The numbering on the Persian Parabellum is military type but uses Farsi figures. The test stamps are "U" with double crown. On certain parts, there is an inspection stamp in the form of a plus sign (+).

SIAMESE CONTRACT

Siam (now Thailand) acquired 150 long Lugers from the Mauser factories in 1936, and 200 P.08 standard pistols in 1937. All the known long Lugers have the date "1936" on the chamber, whereas the short models can have either "1936" or "1937." Their toggle has "Mauser Banner," and at the rear of the frame there is a registration number in Thai figures, a stamp representing a small head of a lion, and a circular stamp probably added by the Thai police. The serial numbers of these pistols are followed by the letter "v."

MILITARY PRODUCTIONS

After being named chancellor of the Reich in 1933, Adolf Hitler got rid of the restrictions imposed on Germany by the Treaty of Versailles and worked quickly to implement the program of rearmament that his policy advocated.

The Reichswehr, a professional army whose numbers were limited to 100,000 men, was replaced by an army of conscription in 1934: the Wehrmacht, with a mission of adding and instructing all recruits of mobilizable units every year.

To equip the large numbers of this new army, an unprecedented effort was required from the weapons factories. As far as Luger pistols are concerned, it is estimated that more than 900,000 P.08 weapons were made for the German army between 1934 and 1942.

Concerning handguns, even though research to find a new pistol was set up, the Wehrmacht chose initially to use the P.08: the weapon had proved itself as the majority of active or reserve soldiers had been trained in its use during the First World War or under the Weimar regime. Large quantities of spare parts remained available, and the assembly lines were already operating at Mauser.

Those P.08s produced by Mauser were identical to those produced previously by DWM, the Erfurt[16] arsenal, or Simson. Only two minor modifications were introduced by Mauser in the manufacture of the grip:

16. In fact, the version produced at the end of the First World War, with the new safety formula (n/A =Neuer Art) and the firing pin with milled grooves for the passage of gas and residue. The Wehrmacht conserved the magazine with an aluminum base, adopted around 1923, as well as numbering the left side of the rear toggle pin, adopted around 1930. The reader unfamiliar with these notions will find them detailed in volume 1.

- A dead hole with a diameter of 2 mm was bored on the inside of the shoulder stock groove.[17] This orifice has no functional use on the finished pistol; its use was to facilitate holding the grip during certain finishing phases (particularly the bluing phase).

- The rear of the frame is slightly reinforced, in order to prevent the release of the toggle pin during the recoil of the slide. This modification seems to have appeared around 1934; however, the old-model frames would still be used for the assembly of military and commercial P.08s until around 1937.

From that year, the method of bluing was modified: bluing with a coating identifiable by a white-polish finish on the interior of parts was replaced by a immersion bluing, giving all treated surfaces a glossy-black appearance. Small parts that had been nonblued and annealed yellow up to then were frequently also blued with a black finish. This rule has exceptions, since it was relatively rare on military P.08s after 1937 but very frequent on commercial models, where some batches were sometimes delivered with secondary parts annealed up to the last year of manufacture.

It is possible to encounter P.08s with a frame and slide with a blued coating, and the barrel treated by immersion bluing.

The grip plates are in nonoiled wood, which gives them a lighter tint than on previous versions and makes them just as susceptible to showing dirt. From 1941 onward, the wooden grip plates would gradually be replaced by black plastic ones.

Apart from military test and acceptance stamps, the design of which developed during production, these military P.08s have very particular markings:

Pistol number 653e, bearing the letter "G" on the chamber, indicating the production year of 1935. The grips are in walnut, and small parts are annealed yellow. This example has a frame without rear reinforcement.

Military P.08 no. 752q, dated 1939 (note the difference in lettering between this year and that of the example dated 1936), bearing the marking "S/42" on the toggle. This marking was replaced during 1939 by the marking "42." The grips are in walnut, small parts are blued, and the frame has a rear reinforcement.

- a toggle marking:
  "S / 42" (with different lettering), used from 1934 to 1939
  "42," used from 1939 to 1941
  "byf" in 1941 and 1942[18]

17. According to Mauser plans seized by the French army, a copy of which is in our possession.

"Eagle 63" acceptance stamps with eagle with lowered wings used by Mauser from the end of 1935 to the beginning of 1937 (here on a 1936 specimen)

P.08 in action during maneuvers of the Wehrmacht on the eve of the Second World War. *ECPA*

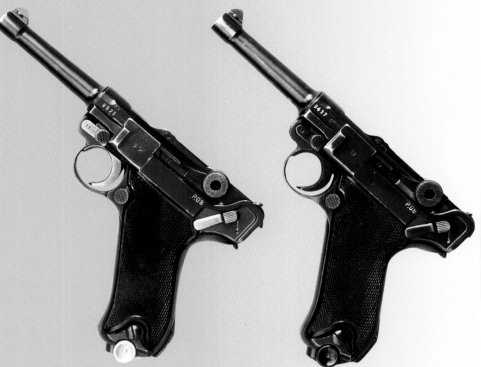

Comparison between two P.08s made in 1941: one with small parts yellowed, the other with blued small parts. These variants have frames marked "P.08."

Comparison between two types of graphics of the date "41" on the chamber of two Mauser-made P.08s

Example 1012b, dated 1939. The toggle is marked with a new Mauser code adopted that year: "42." The grip plates are in walnut; the small parts are blued. This example has a frame with a rear frame reinforcement.

Two different graphics of the code "S/42" on two P.08s made in 1934: a Gothic letter "S" on the example marked 6950 and in Latin on no. 9524.

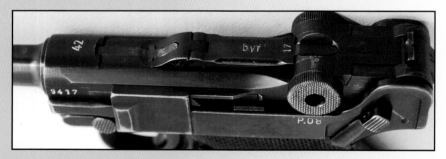

Another example from 1941 (no. 9417f), with a toggle marked with the new code adopted in 1941 for Mauser: "byf," which was to be used until the end of the mass production of the P.08 the following year. On this example, the grip plates are in plastic.

stamped in four figures, but the following years have only two figures:[20] 41, 42.

Mauser interrupted the manufacture of its P.08 in 1942, in order to devote itself exclusively to the P.38. The last German military P.08s were delivered to Portugal. Apparently, a small last batch was transferred to Bulgaria.

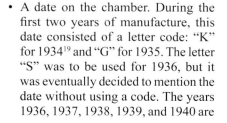

• A date on the chamber. During the first two years of manufacture, this date consisted of a letter code: "K" for 1934[19] and "G" for 1935. The letter "S" was to be used for 1936, but it was eventually decided to mention the date without using a code. The years 1936, 1937, 1938, 1939, and 1940 are

18. This is the general rule. Some P.08s fitted with toggles with a code corresponding to a date earlier than the date of production on the chamber have been observed. This most likely concerns assemblies made from remaining spare parts.
19. The markings P.08 "date K" were made with different types of lettering: roman or Gothic.
20. Unlike the P.08s of the police, on which the years 1941 and 1942 appear in four figures.

Comparison of two sizes of chamber: 1941 (in four figures) and 1940

Another P.08 military Mauser no. 9524, on which the letter "S" of the toggle code is in the Latin alphabet. The code "S/42" was to be used by Mauser up to 1939. After the definitive choice of the Latin alphabet for the letter "S," the shape and size of the number "42" in relation to the letter underwent several variations, until the code was abandoned in 1939. Here the "S" is a little larger than the number, and the "4" is closed. The plates are in walnut and the smalls parts are annealed yellow. As on all the military P.08s made that year, it has a reinforcement of the rear frame ("Mauser Backe").

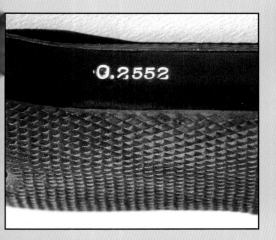

Marking "0" (Baltic Fleet) on the front of the grip of a P.08 belonging to the Kriegsmarine

Weapon no. 8525m, made in 1936. Note the particular graphic style of the figures of 1936, which are found only for that year. On the toggle, the "S" is the same size as the figure "42," and the "4" is open. The small parts are annealed yellow. This example has a frame with no rear reinforcement.

Example bearing the serial no. 8877q, made in 1941 and still with a toggle with the code "42" and therefore often called "41 / 42" by collectors. The marking P.08 was stamped just above the grips on the left side of the frame from 1941 on these weapons.

Another stamp (this time on the rear of the grip) of another navy P.08, belonging to the North Sea fleet

Marking "S/42" accompanied by the real caliber of the barrel (measured on groove valleys) on a replacement barrel. The serial number was not transferred onto this part after its assembly.

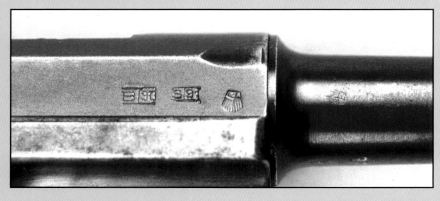

Acceptance stamps made by military inspectors attached to the Mauser factory on some military P.08 Mausers made in 1934 (date K): B/90 and S/91. Other P.08s of the same year bear identically shaped stamps with references Ö/37 and s/92. On the slide and on the right side of the barrel, military test stamps used at this time can be seen: an eagle with dropped wings. The eagle is in a vertical position on the slide and horizontal on the barrel. This test stamp is also on the bolt head on the left side of this part. It was to be used with minor variations in the design until 1939. The various parts of the first P.08 date "K" made (until the number 9100, approximately) are marked with stamps representing the letter "S" (Gothic at the beginning, then Latin).

Several P.08s made for the Wehrmacht: no. 6950, dated "K" (1934), with "S/42" marking in Gothic; number e, dated "G" (1935); number 9417f, dated 42, toggle marked "byf." This example with small blued parts has grips in plastic and a Haenel magazine with a magazine bottom in plastic, no. 8525m, dated 1936, toggle marked "S/42" with the marking "O 2552" at the rear of the grip, indicating that this weapon was used by the Baltic fleet (O = Ostsee) of the Kriegsmarine. Apart from the Wehrmacht belt and various insignia (winter campaign medal, wound badge in bronze, eagle cap badge), the accessories include an army-type fawn holster, a metal cleaning rod, two boxes for sixteen 9 mm cartridges (with the one at the bottom an end-of-war make marked with a stamp: "date of manufacture and origin of powder unknown"), and a takedown and loading tool stamped by the Waffenamt bureau of the Mauser factory.

Acceptance stamps W/154 and S/92, on a P.08 made in 1935 (chamber marked "G"). B/90 and S/91 marks can also be found at the beginning of 1935, which were already used the previous year. During this year, stamps representing small stylized eagles above the figures "211" and "63" appeared.

Acceptance stamps "Eagle 63" with horizontal wings used by Mauser from 1937 to 1939. The military test stamp is also an eagle with horizontal wings holding a swastika in a laurel wreath in its claws. This stamp started to replace the test stamp representing a stylized eagle with drop wings during 1939.

"Eagle 655" acceptance stamps used by Mauser from 1939 to 1941

"Kü" marking. Several P.08s bearing Mauser military markings presenting inspection stamps seem to be those of the Luftwaffe. These weapons are marked with the initials "Kü" on the left side of the slide. These initials were interpreted as being an abbreviation of "Küstenfliegerstaffel": Coastal Flying Squadron. These units were tasked with the mission of reconnaissance and rescue, but it is not possible to establish with certainty whether they received a quantity of Lugers with particular markings. Even though this interpretation is contested today, there is not a more convincing one concerning the presence of these stamps and the letters "Kü" on some P.08s.

P.08 serial number 2749 with "Kü" marking

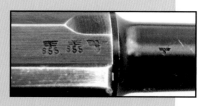

"Eagle 135" acceptance stamps used by Mauser in 1941 and 1942

Luftwaffe-type acceptance stamp (eagle with lowered wings) on the right side of the slide on a P.08 no. 2749 with "Kü" marking

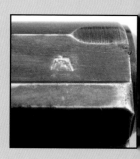

CHAPTER 2

THE KRIEGHOFF LUGER

A Dornier Do 17 returning from a mission. This photo, one of many of the 1939–40 period, clearly shows that at the beginning of the war, heavy bomber crews wore the P.08 in a belt holster. It appears that crews preferred using 7.65 mm caliber pistols in single- or two-seater craft, since they were less bulky in this restricted environment. *ECPA*

The DWM P.08 reconditioned by Krieghoff generally has a serial number followed by a letter "I."

Although the majority of P.08s made in Germany during the Second World War came from the Mauser factories at Oberndorf, a second factory, Heinrich Krieghoff, also made the P.08 under the Third Reich.

Established in the manufacturing town of Suhl in Thuringe, the Krieghoff firm had enjoyed an excellent reputation for its high-quality hunting rifles for many years. Between the wars, the company had diversified its activities by making machine tools for automobiles and selling P.08s that it had assembled from parts surplus from the war. These P.08s, mostly with a toggle marked DWM and a serial number followed by the letter "I," had the trademark of the company at the rear of the frame.

Starting in 1936, Krieghoff received a contract for the manufacture of 10,000 P.08 pistols from the Luftwaffe.

Although the relatively simple assembly and finish procedures for the P.08 that Krieghoff had carried out previously required only the minimum of equipment, the mass production of new weapons represented a considerable effort as regards new equipment, which at first sight appeared quite disproportionate compared to the number of pistols ordered by the Luftwaffe. The decision taken by Krieghoff to undertake this apparently unprofitable operation still generates many questions among amateur weapons collectors today:

1. *Why didn't the Luftwaffe order the P.08 from Mauser, the principal manufacturer?*

As has been discussed in the previous chapter, Mauser was confronted with very many orders for military equipment from 1934, from field guns to light weapons, in particular MG34 machine guns, K98k carbines, and HSc and P.08 pistols.

Despite the opening of a new manufacturing site at Berlin-Borsigswalde, production was not enough for the needs of the German army, which had been given priority of new weapons.

This explains why the Kriegsmarine, Luftwaffe, and Waffen-SS had to find other sources of supply: reusing First World War weapons (with or without reconditioning), calling on other enterprises (German or foreign), and large-scale use of foreign equipment (Austrian from 1937 onward, Czech from 1938 onward, and captured weapons from conquered European countries starting in 1940).

In this context, it is hardly surprising that the Luftwaffe addressed another supplier when Mauser failed to meet its deadlines.

It is possible that the weapons ministry encouraged the opening of another site for manufacturing handguns in the eastern part of the Reich. The Mauser factories at Oberndorf, near the French border, were likely to be subject to aerial attacks or even threatened by a French land offensive. It was wise, therefore, to create a second site of manufacture with 9 mm caliber pistols.

2. Why did the Luftwaffe need so many P.08s?

The Luftwaffe had considerable need of hand weapons: to arm aircrew, and infantry weapons of all types to equip men who protected air bases as well as for antiaircraft artillery units and parachutists who were attached to the Luftwaffe.

Because of its recent creation and its rapid rise in power, the Luftwaffe did not have previously constituted stocks of equipment (either officially or unofficially) before 1934. It was therefore necessary to acquire equipment as rapidly as possible, since it was one of the first elements of the Wehrmacht to participate in a conflict. In 1936, Germany started to engage the Legion Condor, composed mostly of aviators, in Spain. Upon the declaration of war, the ground troops were lacking weapons, and this was resolved by the use of a considerable part of weapons seized from the former Austrian army after the annexation of this country into Germany in 1937. After 1940, the Luftwaffe had K.98k (G98/40) carbines assembled on its behalf at Steyr from spare parts seized in Poland, and the Luftwaffe subcontracted the production of 7.65 mm caliber pistols in Hungary.

3. What reasons incited Krieghoff to engage in the manufacture of the P.08 for the Luftwaffe?

American collector and author Randall Gibson, in his book *The Krieghoff Parabellum*, puts forward an interesting hypothesis: perhaps Heinrich Krieghoff knowingly started this production of P.08s at a loss, with the idea of attracting the favor of the Luftwaffe and proving the technical know-how of his company in order to obtain the concession of the market for the manufacture of MG15 aircraft machine guns, a task for which they were in the running.

Luftwaffe inspectors who examined the P.08 made at Krieghoff were able to observe that the refusal rate of parts was much less compared to Mauser, meaning that quality control was very effective. This was an extremely important criterion for the manufacture of weapons destined for use

in the air, since the conditions of use at high altitude required error-free functionality.

If this hypothesis is correct, the strategy at Krieghoff would have been considered a success, since this enterprise became the main supplier of MG15 aircraft machine guns for German aviation—an eminently more fruitful market than the contract to supply the P.08. Subsequently, Krieghoff was tasked with the manufacture of other weapons for the Luftwaffe, in particular flare pistols, then the FG42 assault rifle.

Luftwaffe poster with safety instructions for loading the P.08: "Point downward when loading, then no one gets hurt!" *Poster Stephane Cailleau / Photo: Marc de Fromont*

"Heinrich Krieghoff" marking stamped on the rear of a P.08 assembled for commercial use from DWM parts by the Krieghoff factory between the wars

Luftwaffe pilot carrying out firing practice with the P.08. *Stephane Cailleau*

Some P.08s made by Krieghoff for the Luftwaffe: code "S" (corresponding to production from the beginning of 1936); serial number 85 (this example has wooden grip plates), dated 1944; serial number 1125◄ (plates in black plastic), dated 1936; serial number 7469 (plates in brown plastic), dated 1940; serial number 10253 (plates in brown plastic)

- The Simson company,[1] near the site of the Krieghoff factory in Suhl, made the P.08 up to the year 1933. After the nationalization of this factory by the Nazis, the majority of spare parts remaining on-site were retrieved by Mauser. The machine tools of the former Simson factory, on the other hand, were still at Suhl at the time when Krieghoff started its dealings with the Luftwaffe.[2] The possibility of being able to reutilize the machinery at Simson must have had a favorable impact on the choice made by Krieghoff to supply the P.08 to the Luftwaffe. In fact, this calculation proved to be deceptive: the machines coming from the former Simson establishment were mostly in bad condition and worn (it should be noted that Simson himself had retrieved them from the Erfurt arsenal after 1918), and a lot of equipment had to be replaced.

5. *Was the P.08 used by aircrew?*

Photos from the first years of the war show that the P.08 was indeed carried in a standard belt holster during flight by some bomber crews.

In addition, some Luftwaffe parachute or flight suits had a special pocket to carry a pistol.

However, the majority of flying personnel seem to have preferred carrying 7.65 mm pistols, less voluminous than the P.08 and just as well adapted to the role of a self-defense weapon for a pilot in enemy territory or for crews based in occupied countries.

During the war, the Luftwaffe also received a large number of P.08s made by Mauser, along with other types of weapons. The deliveries of the P.08s made by Krieghoff are estimated to represent only 3 percent of the total of pistols of all types used during the Second World War by the Luftwaffe.[3]

4. *Why the P.08?*

Although it is understandable that the Luftwaffe needed 9 mm caliber pistols for some of its units, it is somewhat surprising that it chose to have the P.08 made: an old model, difficult to machine, especially for a company that, unlike Mauser, had not recovered all the machinery from previous production lines.

Two explanations can be put forward:

- First, when the contract for the supply of 10,000 P.08s was placed between Krieghoff and the Luftwaffe, the research that led to the adoption of the P.38 was far from being concluded. The mass production of this pistol could not really start until 1940.

1. For more details on this enterprise: see volume 1.
2. At that time, the Simson company had been nationalized: BSW; following this, the majority of its installations and equipment were bought by another Suhl firm, Wilhelm Gustloff.
3. Jan C. Still, *Third Reich Lugers*, 260.

This photo taken on the Eastern Front shows soldiers handling their P.08s with a cord before leaving on a mission. *DR*

This photo shows the adjustment of an equipment strap on a Luftwaffe crew member. A P.08 carried in the left chest pocket can be seen (*circled*); a hole was made in the bottom of the pocket to allow the barrel to stick out horizontally. *DR*

6. Can the granting of the contract for the manufacture of the P.08 destined for the Luftwaffe to Krieghoff be considered as a personal favor for Hermann Göring?

It has often been mentioned that the awarding of the P.08 contract to Krieghoff was due to the fact that the commander in chief of the Luftwaffe, Hermann Göring, was a shareholder of the company. In 1936, he was put in charge of the four-year plan designed to increase the production of weapons and to prepare the German economy for war. That same year, Göring had created the "Reichswerke AG Erzbegau und Eisenhüten Hermann Göring," more commonly known under the name "Hermann Göring Werke" (HGW), which brought together numerous companies involved in weapons manufacturing. In 1939, the HGW held 53 percent of Rheinmetall Borsig and 28 percent of Steyr Daimler Puch and controlled (or was linked with them by bilateral agreements) foreign companies likely to supply raw materials to the Reich during wartime: in Turkey, Finland, Spain, Yugoslavia, and Romania.

It is certain, therefore, that Göring had the possibility to exert some influence on the majority of German firms involved in weapons manufacturing, because of his various roles. It has never been established, however, whether he had any part in Krieghoff's finances. In addition, as has already been mentioned, the concession for the supply of the P.08 to the Luftwaffe was not lucrative for the company.

It is certain that several P.08s received a luxurious finish (engraved, gilded, or silver-plated) before being offered to senior members of the Reich by Krieghoff. Two of these weapons at least were presented to Göring. As fabulous as it may seem to collectors today, these weapons were in fact a fairly modest gift for a person of Göring's status. Their existence does not lead to the conclusion that Göring gave preferential treatment to Krieghoff in any way.

PRODUCTION OF THE P.08 AT KRIEGHOFF

In 1934, Krieghoff received a contract for the manufacture of 10,000 P.08s from the Luftwaffe. The realization of this contract took place during the years 1935, 1936, and 1937.

It is likely that Krieghoff, taking advantage of the fact that the production line had started, made more parts than were required by the Luftwaffe contract.

Throughout the conflict, Krieghoff continued to use the remainder of spare parts made before the war in addition to those made for the original order to assemble small quantities of the P.08, principally for the Luftwaffe as well as a very small number for sale to private individuals.

Upon the declaration of war, there remained a sufficient number of parts at Krieghoff to allow for the assembly of around 3,500 P.08s.

From 1940 onward, the Luftwaffe ordered 1,000 P.08s from Krieghoff, and during the rest of the conflict small numbers of P.08s were delivered intermittently.

Although no known Mauser P.08 has a date after 1942, on the chambers of Krieghoff Lugers the years up to 1945 can be seen.

Up until the collapse of the Third Reich, the Suhl firm also continued to exhaust the remainder of its supply of spare parts to assemble the P.08 either for sale in the civilian sector or to respond to orders from the Luftwaffe. These deliveries would continue until the end of the war.

In the months following the arrival of American troops at Suhl, several P.08s were assembled from the last parts in stock to be sold as souvenirs to the Allied soldiers.

23) Cf. Jan C. Still « Third Reich Lugers » page 260.

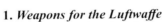

VARIANTS IN MANUFACTURE

Krieghoff P.08s are distinct from those made by Mauser in several respects:

- The frame does not have a rear reinforcement ("Mauser Backe") or the orifice in the shoulder stock groove, which featured on the majority of Mauser-made P.08s.

Mauser used a double type of toggle marking:

- the Mauser logo ("Mauser Banner") for weapons destined for the civilian sector

- a code ("S/42" initially, then "42," then "byf") for weapons destined for the army

Krieghoff marked all its toggles with its commercial logo and never used the code "fzs" for the P.08s that it had been allocated, which was stamped on the other weapons made by Krieghoff for the Luftwaffe (flare pistols, aircraft machine guns, etc.).

1. *Weapons for the Luftwaffe*

The Luftwaffe absorbed the majority of the P.08s made by Krieghoff, and they were distinct from commercial models by the presence of

- a date on the chamber

- test stamps representing an eagle with lowered wings on the left side of the bolt, on the right side of the slide, and under the barrel

- military inspection stamps "Eagle/2" on the majority of parts

Chamber markings

At the very beginning of production, the chamber of the Krieghoff P.08s was marked (as were those of the first Mauser-made P.08s) with a letter code, indicating the year of leaving the factory:

- "G" for 1935
- "S" for 1936

The letter "S" is stamped only on the first pistols delivered in 1936.

During this year, the coding for the year of manufacture was aban-

Toggle marking with the Krieghoff logo and the marking "SUHL" on a P.08 from the first makes of 1936 (code "S" on the chamber)

Toggle marking with the Krieghoff logo and the complete marking "KRIEGHOFF SUHL" on a Luger with a chamber marked "36"

"Eagle/2" stamp on a magazine bottom

doned, and the exit date was then clearly marked in one of two ways:

- for a short time by using the last two figures of the year: "36"

- until the end of the year by the complete marking: "1936"

From 1936 to 1945 the years would be marked using four numbers.

While the dates on the chamber were stamped very deeply on the Mauser P.08, they are very thin and shallow on the Krieghoff, a feature of the marking of the dates that is found at Suhl until the end of production.

Toggle markings
There are two variants of toggle markings on Krieghoff P.08s:

- The first and the most common consists of the marking "Krieghoff Suhl" above the company logo.

- The second, which is rarer, essentially on the productions of 1935 and 1936, has the logo over the inscription "Suhl."

In addition, the detailed study of toggle markings shows some variations in the respective positioning of the different elements, as well as the thickness of the figures. Despite the low number of weapons made, several dies appear to have been used to mark the toggles.

Inspection and test stamps
The examples destined for the Luftwaffe have inspection stamps representing eagles with lowered wings, often with a letter "L" and a figure "2," intertwined with the "L" or positioned under the stamp.

During the course of the war, a simplification of the graphic design can be seen on the inspection stamp "Eagle/2."

It should be noted that the stamp "Eagle/2" is not specific to the Krieghoff factory: these are found on equipment made by other firms, such as magazines for seventy-five cartridges for MG15 aircraft machine guns made by the firm BSW, also set up in Suhl in the former premises of Simson & Co. It can be supposed that the various "Eagle/2" stamps are those of the inspection bureau of the Luftwaffe set up in the town of Suhl.

All secondary parts of the mechanism are also struck with minuscule "Eagle/2" stamps, attesting their conformity after Luftwaffe inspection.

Numbering
Serial numbers of the Krieghoff Luger made from 1935 to 1945 went beyond the number 13000, but it seems that certain numbers were not used.

Grip plates
The grip plates in checkered wood were replaced by molded grip plates in brown plastic in 1937, then by black plastic ones at the end of 1939 or early 1940. Several molds producing a fine checkering were used, followed by those with a wider checkering.

Finish
The polishing of P.08 parts delivered until 1939 was very well done, and their bluing therefore gave a shiny black appearance. From 1940 onward, the polishing was slightly less well done, giving a duller appearance.

Early-type stamp on a 1936 Krieghoff

Another variant of marking with two stamps on a Krieghoff P.08 from 1936

Slide marking on a 1940 Krieghoff. There is a development in the design, and in particular a simplification of the second eagle. The inspection stamps on the frame and the test stamps on the barrel are clearly visible.

"Eagle/2" stamp on a tool

The majority of small parts (trigger, safety lever, locking bolt, ejector) are polished then yellowed during annealing; the magazine catch is annealed blue, which was a feature particular to Krieghoff-produced weapons. (On the Luger made by DWM, Erfurt, and Simson, this part was yellowed. At Mauser, they can be seen with a yellow or blued finish.)

2. Commercial versions

It is estimated that around 1,400 P.08s were assembled by Krieghoff for commercial sale. The majority have a standard finish and are mounted with a 10 cm barrel and chambered for 7.65 mm ammunition and (more commonly) 9 mm Parabellum. However, several very rare examples with a 15 cm barrel have been identified.

These weapons benefit from the same finish as the military models (see previous paragraph). Some rare examples, as has been mentioned previously, destined for personalities of the regime received a luxury silver- or gold-plated finish after engraving. These are without doubt the only Lugers

ever to be engraved. Examples destined for commercial sale are distinct from military models by the following:

- the presence of civilian test stamps (letter "N" strangely positioned horizontally and not vertically, topped with a wreath until 1939, then with an eagle with outstretched wings)

- Some examples have small stamps representing the initials HK (sometimes in a circle).

- a serial number preceded by the letter "P" (for "Privat": destined for sale in the private sector)

- the absence of a date on the chamber

Even though these are not weapons destined for the Luftwaffe, some parts of these weapons bear types of Luftwaffe "Eagle/2" proof marks in different forms. This curiosity is explained by the fact that parts taken from stocks of spares destined for the assembly of military P.08s had sometimes been used for the assembly of civilian weapons (perhaps parts with slightly different dimensions, which even though perfectly functional were without the interchangeability required for military use).

In addition, some of these pistols were marked on the left side of the frame:

HEINRICH
KRIEGHOFF
WAFFENFABRIK
SUHL

Commercial stamp on the Krieghoff P.08 no. P 1196

Serial no. commercial "P 1196" on a P.08 Krieghoff

Undated chamber on a commercial example

Example of a lateral marking

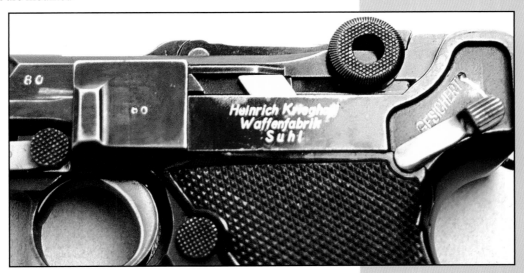

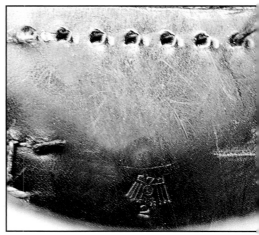

nonexposed sides of the parts. Other examples however, had the serial number composed of three large figures stamped on the left side of the slide.

The first toggles assembled still have the Krieghoff logo, but later ones are sometimes without any markings. Weapons of this serie have also been seen with a small stamp representing the letters "HK" in a circle on the chamber or the toggle.

In order to manage the assembly of complete weapons, the workers at Krieghoff did not hesitate to use parts that were outside the range of tolerance had been discarded for military production, or were coming from other manufacturers (Simson or Mauser), to compensate for the lack of certain Krieghoff-made parts.

ACCESSORIES
Holsters
The Luger Krieghoff was housed in a standard military-type holster. The holsters delivered to the Luftwaffe were most commonly in brown leather, as the rules dictated. The "Eagle/2" proof mark of the Luftwaffe can sometimes be seen on the inside of certain holsters. These marks are minuscule and very lightly marked and therefore can easily be missed.

Superb photo of a gunner, taken onboard a Focke-Wulf Fw 200 "Condor." The man is using an MG15 machine gun and has a P.08 holster on his belt. Perhaps both weapons come from the Krieghoff factory?

3. End-of-war assemblies
For a short time, the Krieghoff factory was authorized to assemble P.08 parts still available after the arrival of American troops at Suhl, in order to satisfy the appetite for souvenirs.

It is estimated that around 250 P.08s were mounted by Krieghoff during this period. These weapons sometimes had numbers only on the

Krieghoff commercial weapon marked "Germany" (weapon destined for export)

CHAPTER 3

THE AFTERMATH OF THE WAR

O n April 20, 1945, the first parts of Lattre's army penetrated the small town of Oberndorf, the home of the Mauser factories. Disappointment awaited the men who entered the factories: nothing remained in the buildings apart from three .22 LR carbines and spare parts!

THE P.08S ASSEMBLED IN FRENCH-CONTROLLED MAUSER FACTORIES

During the following weeks, the totality of finished weapons had left the factory: distributed to German fighting units and Volkssturm militia or hidden with the idea of creating a new resistance. Just like the souvenir hunters, the teams whose mission was to capture any scientific or technological element of interest arrived too late: the most-interesting information and equipment had disappeared. After a swift investigation, it was discovered that the majority of archives and prototypes had been loaded on a special train[1] to try to reach the Bavarian Alps, where the leaders of the Reich still hoped to constitute a last bastion of resistance.

Several weeks later, Germany surrendered. The victors divided their territories into different zones of occupation. The province of Württemberg, where the town of Oberndorf was situated, was placed under French control.

In August 1945, the French command ordered the resumption of activities at the Mauser factory. Seemingly, the work carried out under the control of the French administration was restricted to repairing weapons captured on the ground and to

A French soldier in Germany proudly showing off a P.08, with its holster attached to his US belt. *ECPA*

the assembly of several thousand others from the many spare parts available on-site.

These activities continued until May 1946. At the end of this period, in application of the interallied agreements, all weapons production on German soil had to stop and the weapons factories had to be dismantled. A decision by the administrator general of the French military government, dated the November 5, 1947, ordered the breakup of the Mauser establishment, the dispersal of the machines,[2] and the destruction of the buildings.

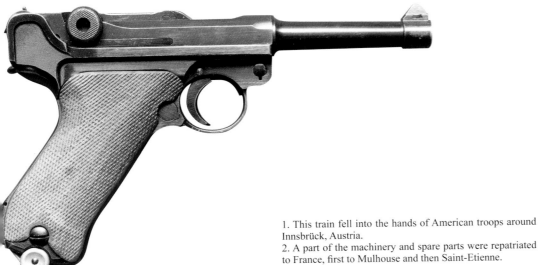

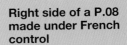

Right side of a P.08 made under French control

1. This train fell into the hands of American troops around Innsbrück, Austria.
2. A part of the machinery and spare parts were repatriated to France, first to Mulhouse and then Saint-Etienne.

French holster for a long P.08, accompanied by a lanyard

An unusual holster, with a press stud on the inside flap

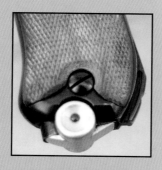

P.08s made under French control were principally originally fitted with two Haenel-type magazines, with a blued body, without markings, and with an aluminum base simply struck with the serial number and held in place by a blued pin. Subsequently, all sorts of other recovered or salvaged magazines were able to be used with these weapons.

The valuable testimony of August Weiss[3] gave an initial assessment of the importance of the assembly of weapons carried out under French control.

Mr. Weiss estimated that the production of weapons from the Mauser factories between August 1945 and May 1946 amounted to the following:

- 47,696 98k carbines

- 6,375 .22 LR carbines

- 3,500 P.38s

- 20,000 HsC pistols

- 2,560 P.08s

Mauser factory production tables showed the assembly of 3,476 P.08s between June 1945 and April 1946. These two sources therefore make it possible to quantify the number of P.08s assembled under French control to be in the region of 2,500 to 3,500.

FEATURES OF THE P.08S ASSEMBLED UNDER FRENCH CONTROL

Dimensions

The P.08 pistols were to be assembled by the French army from spare parts stocked from the time the production of this weapon was stopped in 1942. Two variants were made:

- long P.08 with 20 cm barrel, for a few rare examples

- standard P.08 with 10 cm barrel for the majority of the pistols manufactured

The reassembly of these long P.08s can appear surprising; this type of weapon does not correspond at all to the standards of combat pistols as they were designed in 1945.[4]

The memoirs of veterans establish that the rare long pistols produced were essentially destined for French or foreign soldiers wishing to acquire a P.08 for individual use or to be given to visiting personalities.[5] The fact that some of these weapons were accompanied by a luxury stock, reminiscent of those pistol carbines from the beginning of the century, with the basic wooden plate of the regulation long Luger, would tend to confirm this hypothesis of a vocation outside the military.

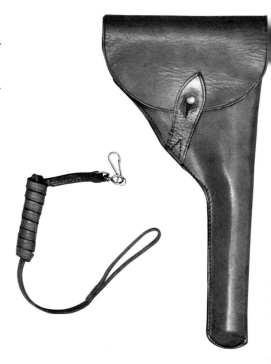

Finish

The pistols examined all have an entirely blued finish, done by immersion of all the parts with the exception of the firing pin and the safety.

The finish of these weapons is identical to that of the Mauser commercially made P.08 from

3. After being employed by DWM during the First World War, the late August Weiss was hired by Mauser between the wars. He was director of production for handguns in this company until 1945. The very accurate memories he has of this period were collected by several weapons historians, in particular Fred Datig and Reinard Kornmayer. The testimony of Mr. Weiss greatly contributed to the enrichment of knowledge concerning P.08 production at Mauser.
4. These P.08s are referenced in the French army under the classification number 151.311.300.100 and the code number E.M.A. 1 113 41. These numbers cover the 10 cm long barrel and what French documentation considers two derivative versions: a model with a long barrel and type LP 08 adjustable sight, and a model known as "medium barrel" that we have not been able to identify.
5. This is asserted by a letter addressed to NAPCA in November 1991 by Dwight Crandell of Lakewood, Colorado. He was assigned to the 100th US Infantry Division after 1945, stationed in the region of Stuttgart, and reported that subject to a permit issued by the French army services of Karlsruhe (whose attribution, he pointed out, was greatly facilitated by the presence of several spare parts for Jeeps), it was possible for the occupying troops to acquire brand-new P.08s made at Mauser by the French army. The author of the letter indicates that he traveled to Oberndorf, where he bought twelve P.08s for him and other officers of his unit, half of which had a short barrel and the other half a long barrel, for the price of six dollars apiece. He later brought two of these Lugers back to the United States: one long and one short.

941 to 1942. The polishing, less thorough than re-1939, left traces of machining, clearly visible nder the glossy-black bluing. These pistols have heckered grips in light wood (probably beech).

Some of these weapons were phosphate oated or mounted with different grips after their econditioning in French military establishments.

Magazine

.08s assembled under French control were enerally fitted with a Haenel-type magazine (see he chapter dedicated to magazines at the end of nis special edition). The magazine frames are lued and, unlike those from the war production, ave no markings.

The magazine followers were made according o the availability of pressed or machined parts.

The magazine bottoms are in aluminum (and ot plastic) and simply have the weapon number.

It should also be pointed out that France lanned to restart production of magazines to eplace the defective magazines of its P.08s. Since he manufacturing process of the Haenel/ chmeisser-type magazine was not adapted to nake a small series, another process was used. Vhile conserving the outline of the Haenel nagazine body, whose robustness was entirely atisfactory, another process of welding on the ear side of the magazine was envisaged. This rocess went under the name of "the Levallois roject" in French military archives exhumed by jeorges Machtelinckx, in the form of plans marked Mulhouse arsenal.

In the "Levallois project," the connection of ne two sides of the folded metal sheet making p the body of the magazine was carried out in ne following manner: A rectangle of 8 mm wide heet metal, 121.4 to 121.7 mm long and 0.4 mm nick, is positioned inside the body of the magazine, gainst the rear side. This sheet metal is fixed to oth edges of the rear side of the magazine by vo welding spots.

The total width of the inside of the magazine body (the space separating the rear side from the front side) is about 26.9 mm on German-made magazines. It can be seen on the plans that this dimension is diminished by the presence of this metal, but the space remaining (around 26.65 mm) is within the limits so as not to hinder the movement of the cartridges in the magazine.

This process has the advantage of allowing magazines to be produced in small quantities, so as to respond to occasional needs. We are not aware if magazines were in fact made by this method, however.

Among the many magazines destined for the P.08s made under French control that the authors have been able to examine, none appears to have been made in that way.

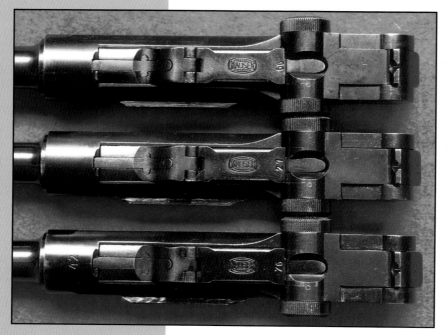

There are chambers without a date or dated 42 on these French P.08s. *From left to right*: the number 2976 on the chamber marked "42," the number "621" on the unmarked chamber, the number "366" on the unmarked chamber

Markings

Three main variants of markings have been identified:

1st variant: P.08 with no German test stamp, chamber undated, toggle marked with "Mauser Banner," with a five-pointed star and a three-figure serial number on the right side of the slide. This number is also at the front of the frame, and the two last numbers are on the main parts of the weapon. The exact meaning of the five-pointed star is not known; it is also found on the P.38 and on some 98k carbines made under French control.

2nd variant: Pistols identical to those previously mentioned, but instead of the star there is a stamp representing an eagle with outstretched wings above a letter "N."[6] This is the mark regularly stamped on weapons produced for sale in the public sector (stamp "Eagle/N") under the Third Reich.

However, on the pistols made during the Nazi period, this stamp was put in three different places:

- on the front side of the front sight base

- on the left side of the bolt head

- on the left side of the slide

On those P.08s assembled under French control, this stamp is found only on the left side of the slide.

While this stamp is generally positioned above the serial number on weapons made under the Third Reich,[7] it is placed in front of this number on the P.08s presumed to be of French manufacture.

3rd variant: These are pistols similar to those of the second variant, but with the year "42" on the chamber.

Numbering

The complete serial number is on the left side of the slide and at the front of the frame. No pistols assembled under French control have a suffix letter, which is normal when we know that the volume of production remained fewer than 10,000, and this quantity was way below the 10,000 pieces required for the use of suffix letter in the numbering.

The last two figures of this number are on all parts except these:

- the extractor

- the barrel

- the bolt head

- the firing pin

- the bolt latch

- the safety lever and the safety piece

During the 1960s, a certain number of French army P.08s were sold to cinema props departments, which then transformed them to fire blanks. Perhaps Lino Ventura is holding one such weapon here? *DR*

6. This letter "N" is the first letter of the word "Nitropulver" or smokeless powder.

7. There are however exceptions to this rule, as proved by the photo of a P.08 1934 commercial Mauser, shown on page 260 of Charles Kenyon's book *Lugers at Random*.

Long P.08 no. 400, made under French control. The weapon is with its stock.

Details on the stock on the long P.08 no. 400

Barrel of East German make, recognizable by the "crowned N" stamp of the Suhl testing stand and by the nonridged sight support.

P.08 serial numbers currently presumed to be made under French control are as follows:

- On pistols with a five-pointed star stamp: 204, 223, 225, 260, 280, 366, 367, 372, 377, 380, 400, 408, 415, 450. Pistols numbered 260, 400, and 450 are long-barrel models.

- On pistols with the commercial "Eagle/N" stamp, with undated chamber: 500, 620, 621, 810, 832, 854, 939, 1018, 1020, 1254, 1649, 1979, 2033, 2584, 2912. Pistols numbered 854, 1649, and 2584 are long-barrel models.

- On pistols with the commercial and the date "42" on the chamber: 2700, 2992, 2976. These three pistols are fitted with the standard 10 cm barrel.

It should be pointed out that the French army also used many other P.08s (officially listed or not): weapons captured from the German army, but also significant numbers of weapons seized from Algerian rebels, who were generously equipped with brand-new German material, Second World War surplus, by international arms traffickers.

A letter addressed to Reinard Kornmayer by the Ministerial Delegation for Armament[8] in 1973 shows that the Gendarmerie Nationale were the last to use the P.08, since the weapon was withdrawn from service in 1970. These P.08s were then kept in army depots.

The majority were destroyed, but a small number were resold at the end of the 1960s to cinema prop departments, which were then transformed to fire blanks only. Some of them were also sold abroad.[9]

THE P.08 VOPO

On October 7, 1949, the Soviet zone of occupation in Germany was constituted in the German Democratic Republic (GDR). The remilitarization of Germany was at that time not permitted by clauses of the armistice; the new republic created a militarized police force to carry out surveillance of the new border and uphold domestic law and order: the Volkspolizei (abbreviated to "Vopo").

During the establishment of this force, the units of the Vopo were armed with weapons of the former Wehrmacht, available in large quantities, and the majority of the new policemen had already been trained in their use prior to 1945. Among these weapons were many P.08s, and after being allocated to the Vopo, they were subject to reconditioning, which gave them very specific features:

- Most had the original barrel replaced by a new one identifiable by the "crowned N" stamp of the Suhl testing stand, placed under the barrel, and by the absence of ridges on the inclined

8. Letter no. 070861, dated January 18, 1973
9. It would appear that during the rearmament of Austria, several batches of weapons of German origin were donated to this country by France, among which were some P.08s possibly coming from this famous series made under French control.

ramp on the foresight base. Some barrels also have the month and year of assembly (e.g., 10-53 for October 1953).

- They have various markings: sometimes new test stamps, almost always with markings showing they belonged to the police: some small stamps representing a crest containing a figure, surrounded by rays and a capital "X."

- They were most often reblued, with a thick glossy bluing over a crude repolishing.

- Their grips were replaced by ones in plastic with tints from dark to reddish brown, with a circular motif at the center.

- Their original magazine was most often replaced by a Haenel-type magazine extruded with the bottom in gray-colored metal. These magazines bear the marking 2/1001, which is a code indicating that they had been made by the VEB Ernst Thälmann Kombinat factory in Suhl, which is none other than the old Haenel factory after its confiscation by the communist authorities and its merger with the former Sauer & Sohn factory.

Apart from the barrels, the grips, and magazines, various spare parts (trigger, trigger side plate, locking bolt) were also manufactured again so as to allow for the repair of damaged weapons. It would seem that the recommencement of complete weapons production was envisaged by the East German authorities. German historian Joachim Görtz[10] points out that a hundred P.08s with the serial number preceded with the letter "N" and marked "1001" at the front of the frame likely constituted the preproduction of this ultimately abandoned project. After the replacement of weapons of the former Wehrmacht by standard weapons of the Warsaw Pact, East Germany supplied a certain number of countries undergoing difficult situations (Ethiopia in particular) with weapons declassified by the Vopo. The GDR soon found that it was advantageous to sell its P.08 supply in Western countries, where collectors enjoyed the availability, since the Vopo used all variants of the P.08 at its disposal, without taking notice of the various markings. Among the weapons acquired in the GDR are some P.08s bearing the "Mauser Banner" marking attributed to the German

10. Joachim Görtz, *Die Pistole 08*, edition 200, op. cit.

Commercial P.08 made in 1940 for the German police, reconditioned after World War II for the People's Police of the German Democratic Republic (Volkspolizei, abbreviated to "Vopo"). The weapon has a new barrel and has been reblued in shiny, thick black, and its grips have been replaced by ones in plastic, with a circular motif in the center. The magazine, also made after the war, has a bottom in gray-colored metal alloy.

"X" marking that can be seen on some reconditioned parts for the Vopo

On this example, no. 2714x, the test stamp Eagle/N can be clearly seen above the serial number (and not in front as on the French P.08). On the other hand, the Vopo inspection stamp has been covered by three figure "8"s superimposed before the weapon was resold on the Western market.

On this P.08 "date G," the number on the toggle has been crudely filed and restruck. The part also has a stamp from the testing stand at Suhl.

Volkspolizei stamp (number in a circle of rays) stamped on the forward of the trigger guard.

P.08 no. 1506 with Austrian marking "BH" (Bundesheer). The numbering without a suffix letter and the position of the "Eagle/N" stamp in front of (and even "in") the number means that these weapons could have been supplied by France to Austria after the war.

Member of a Jewish organization using a long Parabellum during the fighting preceding the creation of the state of Israel in 1948. *DR*

First type of Parabellum Mauser (sometimes called 1970 model). The weapon is still very close to the 1906/29 Swiss Parabellum, whose plans and machinery were used in part to produce it. Note in particular the grip without a relief pattern at the front and bottom, and the simplified outline of the safety and disassembly levers.

Officers of the Norwegian air force practicing firing with a P.08 during the 1970s. *Richard Karlson*

police under the Third Reich. Dutch models, Simsons, and Krieghoffs are all of great interest to Luger collectors, even if the weapons were occasionally repaired using parts that were nonstandard on the initial model.

OTHER VARIATIONS

An Austrian variant: a P.08 with the BH (for "Bundesheer": federal army) stamp under the locking bolt, preceded by a small stamp representing an eagle. These weapons have features very similar to those of the Luger made under French control: the absence of chamber marking, an Eagle/N stamp placed in front of the serial number rather than under it, and a Haenel-type magazine with aluminum bottom and without markings apart from the serial number and fixed to the body by a central bronzed pin. The serial number is without a letter code.

It is possible that these are old P.08s from a batch assembled under French control in 1945–46, transferred to Austria by France during its rearmament.

UTILIZATION BY NORWAY

The Norwegian army used the P.08 until recently, taken from supplies of weapons captured from the Wehrmacht in 1945. It would seem that the Norwegians did not stamp specific markings on their P.08.

THE POSTWAR PARABELLUM MAUSER

The strong demand for Luger pistols on the American market encouraged arms dealer Samuel Cummings, himself a collector of Lugers and one-time president of the Interarms company of Alexandria, Virginia, to contact the Mauser establishment in order to study the possibility of restarting production of this prestigious pistol. Only the return to service of the existing machine tools could allow the manufacture of such a weapon at an acceptable price. The machinery at Oberndorf had been dispersed at the end of the war or destroyed by occupying French forces. The only complete assembly of machine tools and inspection devices still in existence for the production of the Luger remained stocked in the Berne arsenal in Switzerland; however, as a result of this pistol being withdrawn as the regulation weapon in 1947, the arsenal was dismantled.

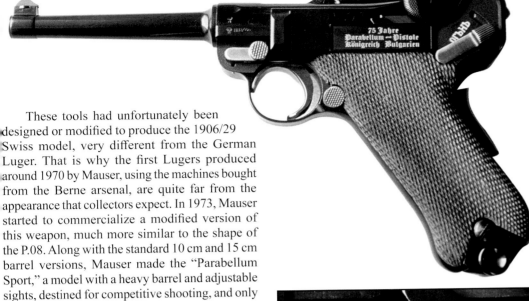

These tools had unfortunately been designed or modified to produce the 1906/29 Swiss model, very different from the German Luger. That is why the first Lugers produced around 1970 by Mauser, using the machines bought from the Berne arsenal, are quite far from the appearance that collectors expect. In 1973, Mauser started to commercialize a modified version of this weapon, much more similar to the shape of the P.08. Along with the standard 10 cm and 15 cm barrel versions, Mauser made the "Parabellum Sport," a model with a heavy barrel and adjustable sights, destined for competitive shooting, and only a very small quantity was made.

Mauser also produced several series limited to 250 weapons, commemorating the most-famous Luger models of the past: Swiss, Bulgarian, Russian, naval, pistol-carbine, 1902 model with cartridge counter, "American Eagle," and seventy-fifth anniversary of the long Parabellum.

To satisfy a clientele that wanted to have the traditional Luger outline, Mauser modified the 1970 model. This model, known as "1973," had a grip, safety, and disassembly levers more in line with the wishes of collectors. Here is a commemorative model from the Bulgarian contract.

Details of the markings on the commemorative Bulgarian model

In addition to the models commemorating historic contracts, there were also models commemorating various events. Here is an example produced in 1990 for the International Arms Fair (IWA) at Nuremberg. Very few of these very costly weapons were made.

The Parabellum Sport: heavy-barrel version, for competitive shooting, developed at the end of the 1970s. The fragility of the adjustable sight led to the production of this version being stopped. A total of 250 specimens in 9 mm or 7.65 mm Parabellum were made, and today the Parabellum Sport is very rare.

Short-barrel Luger in .45 A.C.P. This weapon is made from two Lugers that had been cut and rewelded to obtain a slightly larger weapon, capable of accepting .45 ammunition. A very high-level finish gives the pistol an appearance that is every bit as good (or more so) than that of the best DWM productions. The weapon had a surface bluing. The operation and the accuracy are also irreproachable.

John Vernon Martz: passionate about the Luger mechanism, this former technician in the aeronautic industry produced made-to-measure "Custom Lugers" from his workshop in Lincoln, California, for many years. His weapons are equipped with a patented device allowing the open toggle to be closed by acting on the safety lever: the MSTR or Martz Safe Toggle Release.

Marking of a Luger in .45. The weapon here has received a polished stain finish. The initials JVM of the maker are intertwined in the style of a DWM monogram, and the caliber and the date of manufacture are mentioned, along with the position of the MSTR device.

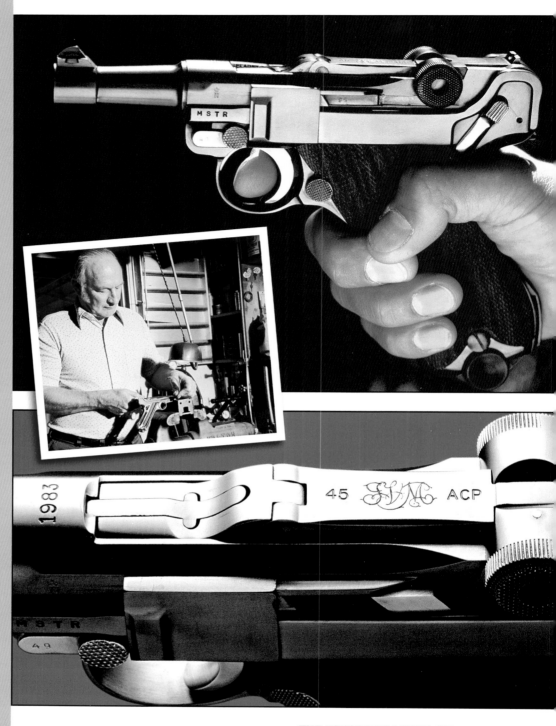

At the beginning of the 1990s, Mauser still assembled several engraved luxury models and some commemorative models, produced on the occasion of the International Arms Fair (IWA) at Nuremberg. The manufacture of the Parabellum Mauser was finally ended in 1999, when the Oberndorf firm definitively abandoned the sports weapons sector to concentrate on heavy armaments. The Parabellum Mauser, for a while not appreciated by purists, began to be sought after by collectors.

THE "CUSTOM" LUGER OF JOHN VERNON MARTZ

We will return to the constant success that Luger had in the American market in the following chapter. Toward the end of the 1970s John Vernon Martz, a former aeronautics technician and expert in machining and welding, took up the challenge of making a .45-caliber Luger. To carry this out, he started with two "standard" 9 mm Lugers that he cut, rewelded, and machined to obtain an oversized grip, slide, and toggle. He fitted a new barrel in .45 caliber and a made-to-measure magazine.

After the development phase, the weapon functioned perfectly, with an accurate and agreeable firing, but principally the finish that Martz gave to these weapons was of the highest order: cleanly polished with sharp angles, this exceptional pistol had a similar appearance to the best productions of the DWM assembly lines prior to the First World War. Martz spent his retirement making custom-made Lugers for wealthy amateurs. The perfect finish was combined with constant research concerning the adaptation of this pistol—reputed to be temperamental—to the most-surprising ammunition. Martz made several Lugers in .38 automatic, and others in 7.63 mm Mauser and in .22 Magnum, which according to him was more difficult than any other caliber he had previously worked with.

A masterpiece: a John V. Martz Luger in .22-caliber Magnum: without doubt one of the most difficult adaptations that he ever made

OTHER LUGER POSTWAR PISTOLS
Surplus P.08s

After several decades during which the Luger had become scarce, several sizable batches arrived in Europe in two waves:

- the Luger resold from 1980 by the German Democratic Republic (GDR)

- Those exhumed from various Russian and Ukrainian arsenals after 1995. These were P.08s captured from the Wehrmacht and kept in Soviet Empire reserves.

Small batches of Lugers resold by Finland or Vietnam (probably examples captured from the French army) can be added to ones captured from the Wehrmacht.

Despite these arrivals, highly appreciated by shooters and collectors, the quantity of surplus Lugers is diminishing constantly, and these types of weapons are becoming ever more rare, particularly specimens in perfect condition. The cost of traditional machining of a Luger at the end of the twentieth century has led to a cost price making this type of weapon difficult to market. The last manufacturer of Parabellum, the Mauser-Werke at Oberndorf, started the new production of the Parabellum in 1970, but this was abandoned at the end of the 1980s.

The Mitchell company decided to relaunch the manufacture of Luger pistols by using more-economical production techniques than those used originally. The many long parts, too expensive to machine, were subject to microfusion.

These stainless-steel pistols are accessible at a reasonable price. They cannot be confused with the Luger made by DWM Simson, Mauser, Krieghoff, or the Berne arsenal, but they nonetheless have an attractive appearance and make firing a Luger possible for enthusiasts without having to use expensive period pieces.

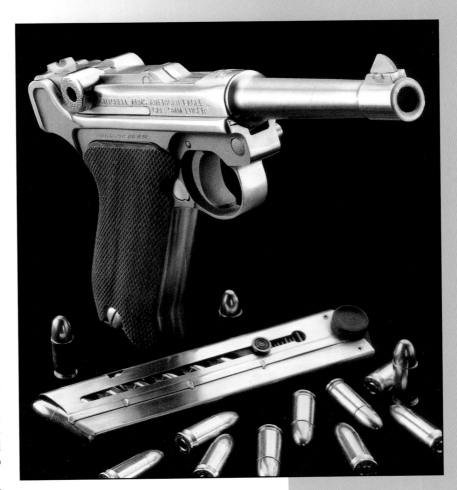

Luger Mitchell

"Waffen Frankonia" stamp on an East German P.08 resold by this company

CHAPTER 4

THE GREAT LUGER FAMILIES

Soldiers of the Swiss army engineers. The man in the center holds a Parabellum. This photo dates from the First World War.
Maurice Sublet

Close-up of the last two figures of the serial number on the right extremity on the disassembly lever: a type of mark that is found on Swiss Luger models 00 and 00/06

Military acceptance mark on the back of the frame.

Inspection stamp "Cross/V" on a 1900 Swiss Parabellum, verified by the inspector Vogelsang. Also visible are the military acceptance stamps (Swiss cross) in front of the inspector's stamp and on the side of the barrel.

Inspection stamp "Cross/V" on an 00/06. The order of stamps is the opposite to that on the previous weapon.

THE SWISS LUGERS

1900 Swiss military model

Between 1893 and 1900, the Swiss army led a campaign of tests to compare the different automatic pistols of the time. The DWM factories initially presented their Borchardt pistol, then, during the years that followed, several other versions that had been improved by George Luger. The intermediary models are generally designated under the name "Borchardt-Luger"; the definitive version adopted by the Swiss federal council on May 4, 1900, is now currently referred to as the "Luger 1900 model" by collectors. Its regulation Swiss name is "Pistolet Parabellum model 00" or "Selbstlade Pistole, Ordonnanz Modell 1900."

A first order of 5,000 Lugers in 7.65 mm caliber Parabellum was addressed to DWM by the Swiss. These weapons differed from the commercial version of the model,[1] sold throughout the world by DWM, by the Swiss cross in a sun in splendor, which was stamped on the chamber, and by military acceptance stamps representing a cross above a letter "V": the initial of the military inspector Vogelsang, in charge of checking the conformity of pistols delivered to Switzerland by DWM.

1. *The Luger: A Legendary Pistol*, vol. 1, pp. 12–14.

RIGHT: Several Parabellum made by the arsenal at Berne: 06/29 no. 62435, 9 mm caliber (with black grips). Above this model is a Swiss military–made box of cartridges for 9 mm caliber pistols, dating from November 1945; 06/29 no. 67580, 7.65 mm caliber (with brown grips); 06/29 no. 51838, 7.65 mm caliber (with red grips); and model 1900 / 06 no. 20535, 7.65 mm caliber.

These first Swiss military Lugers were numbered from 1 to 5,000 and were delivered to the Swiss army in several batches, during which variations appeared on several elements whose exact correlation with serial numbers is not always possible.

Magazine
The catch allowing the operation of the magazine follower is very flat on the first 750 weapons delivered to Switzerland. The thickness of this button would be increased later, and, as a consequence, the depth of the guideway in which it operated would be increased.

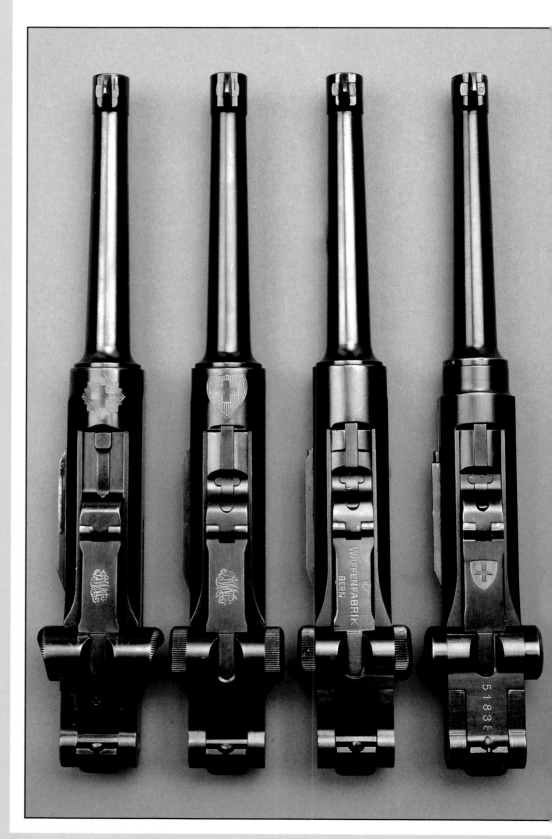

FROM LEFT TO RIGHT: DWM-made model 00, with chamber marked with a cross in a sun in splendor. Note that this example has a reinforced extractor, adopted by the Swiss army around 1920. Model 00/06 made by DWM, bearing the marking "Cross in a blazon" Waffenfabrik Bern–made 00/06 model. Note the particular machining of the bolt head. This model is the first Swiss Luger to have no marking on the chamber. Model 06/29, made by Waffenfabrik Bern. The numerous differences of manufacture that this model has compared to the rest of the Luger family are visible here. *Marc de Fromont*

safety lever

The first version is equipped with a safety lever with an upper part checkered on a length of 3.7 mm. On the second version, this part is checkered to a length of 10 mm, but it is thicker. On the third, the top of the safety lever is merely ridged.

Trigger

The width of this part is considerably increased on weapons with a serial number between 3900 and 5000.

Apart from the 5,000 examples of this first order, DWM addressed a hundred pistols to the Swiss government with a serial number preceded by a letter "E." The reason for this delivery has not been clearly established (weapons delivered for testing or to be given to important figures?). In 1914, these prefix "E" weapons were renumbered from 5001A to 5100A and assigned to the army.

Around 1920, a reinforced extractor was adopted for 1900 models still in service.

Apart from the Lugers delivered to the army, DWM went on to deliver many 1900 models to Swiss armorers, struck with the Swiss emblem for sale to individuals. These commercial examples do not have Swiss military stamps.

In 1906, the Swiss Confederation acquired 10,215 type 1906 Luger pistols, numbered from 5001 to 15215. These were the new model of Luger as proposed by DWM, called the "1906 model." The official designation of the weapon in Switzerland is "Selbstladepistole Ordonnanz, Modell 1900 / 06." There are two variants of this weapon:

- The first is marked, as is the 1900 model, with a cross in a sun in splendor.

- The second is marked with a cross in a crest.

The reason for this change of motif is not known. Principally, the cross motif in a sun in splendor appeared on pistols marked from 5001 to 9000, and the cross-in-a-crest motif is on those numbered from 9001 to 15215.

World War I interrupted deliveries of Luger pistols from Germany to Switzerland, and so it was decided to have this pistol made under license in Switzerland by the arsenal at Berne.

Production did not really begin until November 1918, and it continued until May 1933.

Unidentified stamp in the shape of a shield under the barrel of a Swiss 00/06. This marking appeared on various Parabellums made by DWM before the First World War.

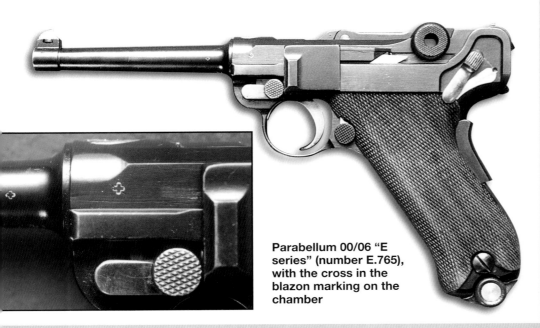

Parabellum 00/06 "E series" (number E.765), with the cross in the blazon marking on the chamber

Markings of an 00/06 "E series" (serial number "E765")

Waffenfabrik Berne logo on the rear of the frame on a 06/29

Swiss noncommissioned officers (NCOs) training between the wars. *Maurice Sublet*

Safety lever on a 06/29

TOP: safety lever springs and extractor on a 1906 made by DWM. BOTTOM: The same parts from a 06/29. The spring is no longer machined but composed of a blade in curved steel. The extractor of the 06/29 was designed to surround its pin.

The Berne arsenal[2] made 17,874 pistols, numbered from 15216 to 33089. These weapons are identifiable by the following features:

- the marking "WAFFENFABRIK BERN," topped by a Swiss cross, stamped on the toggle

- the absence of marking on the chamber

- the grips where the checkering has a smooth zone around the peripheries

- the slight relief at the front of the bolt head

Starting in 1928, a series of tests were led at the Berne arsenal, with the aim of simplifying the manufacture of the Luger pistol and improving its operational safety. This resulted in the adoption of a simplified model the following year, called 1906/29 model "Selbstladepistole Ordonnanz Modell 19 06/29." This variant is distinct due to the following features:

- presence of a pronounced shouldering at the level of the chamber

- protuberance of the trigger side plate extended from top to bottom

- smooth actuator knobs

- simplified safety and disassembly levers

- front side of the grip is straight

2. This version is sometimes called "1924 model" by certai[n] collectors. This name does not appear to have any real basis It seems preferable to conserve the regulation Swiss name o[f] model 00/06 (or even model 1906), sometimes followed b[y] "Manufacture de Berne."

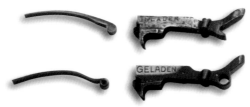

View of the interior of a DWM trigger side plate (1) and the same parts taken from a 06/29. The yellow circle designates the housing machined in the thickness of the plate, to serve as a support for the left extremity of the trigger pin.

This close-up shows the particular shape of the chamber on the 06/29, as well as the simplified safety lever. The Cross/M stamp is that of Colonel Muhlmann, weapons inspector at the Berne factory.

Luger 06/29 serial no. 62435, assembled with a 9 mm Parabellum barrel. During the Second World War, the factory at Berne led tests with the aim of replacing the 7.65 mm by the 9 mm as the handgun caliber. After the war, these tests led to the Parabellum being abandoned in favor of the model 1949 pistol developed by SIG.

Marking on the barrel of the pistol no. 62435 in 9 mm Parabellum

- The magazine bottom plates were originally made from a synthetic resin material in a red-orange color, but this soon proved to be quite fragile and was replaced by a more standard brown and then black plastic.

- the abandonment of the triangular sights in favor of a U-shaped sighting notch and a rectangular front sight

- extended safety lock and the extension of two follower slots penetrating the grip

These pistols were sanded and blued or phosphate-coated matte gray.

The Berne arsenal produced 27,910 type 1906/29 pistols numbered from 50001 to 77941 between 1933 and 1946 for the Swiss army.

A total of 1,917 specimens (identifiable by the letter "P" in front of the serial number) were made for the civilian market, and a final series of 317 pistols were assembled after 1946 from parts remaining in stock for civilian use.

Since the Swiss army had adopted machine pistols in 9 mm caliber Parabellum, they planned to make the ammunition unit by transforming its 06/29 pistols in 9 mm caliber by changing the barrel. This arrangement, applied on several test models, did not become general. Switzerland finally abandoned the Luger in 1949 and adopted the model 1949 pistol in 9 mm Parabellum, proposed by SIG. It was with a model 1906/29 pistol modified by the Berne arsenal that the Swiss policeman Heinrich Keller became the world champion at the military shooting championships in Buenos Aires in 1949; firing the pistol at 50 meters, he scored 559 points out of 600.

- reinforced fixation of the extractor and the trigger; some small internal parts also show simplifications in the machining

- The magazine frame, made from a single piece in chrome-plated steel. The bottom, made of plastic, is fixed by two pins.

Stamp indicating that this part was made by a subcontractor of the SIG firm

Detail of the markings of the 598v pistol. The letter "v" followed by the serial number and the double-crown "U" stamp confirms that this is a production (or assembly) carried out at Mauser.

On the eve of the Second World War, when the Swiss army had already adopted the 06/29, Mauser continued to supply Swiss armorers with standard type Lugers for sale to individuals. Here is the 598v model, still with a DWM toggle even though this is in fact a Mauser-produced weapon.

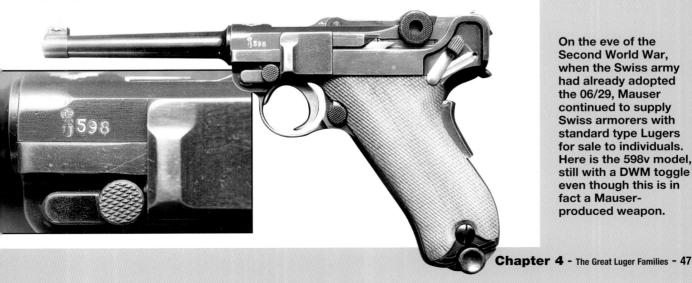

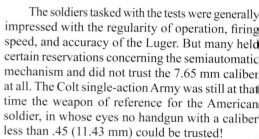

THE AMERICAN EAGLES

Luger 1900 model and the American tests

In March 1901, the Board of Ordnance and Fortifications, responsible for the choice of material in the US Army, asked Hans Tauscher, exclusive DWM agent for the United States, to procure two Luger 1900 pistols along with 2,000 cartridges for preliminary tests.

The series of tests carried out with these two weapons was satisfactory, and Lt. Col. Frank H. Philips, then director of the Board of Ordnance, recommended that the tests be continued and that credit be released for the purchase of 1,000 weapons and 200,000 cartridges, with the intention of proceeding to more-extensive testing and an evaluation by troops.

Having obtained satisfaction, it received a first delivery of 900 weapons (800 according to some sources) from M. Tauscher, with nonconsecutive serial numbers going from 6100 to 7100. Shortly thereafter, a complementary delivery was sent with 100 (200 according to some sources) other pistols bearing serial numbers around 7200. The weapons were addressed to the Springfield arsenal, which inspected them before giving them to the units responsible for tests. A belt holster adapted for this weapon was specially made by the Rock Island arsenal.

Unlike other Luger 1900 models, imported by Tauscher for the American shooter clientele, the Lugers given to the Board of Ordnance in Germany have the marking "GERMANY," usually struck on imported civilian weapons. The pistols delivered for testing were in all points similar to the weapons sold in the civilian sector. In particular, they have the magnificent marking representing the American eagle.

The soldiers tasked with the tests were generally impressed with the regularity of operation, firing speed, and accuracy of the Luger. But many held certain reservations concerning the semiautomatic mechanism and did not trust the 7.65 mm caliber at all. The Colt single-action Army was still at that time the weapon of reference for the American soldier, in whose eyes no handgun with a caliber less than .45 (11.43 mm) could be trusted!

The results of these tests were communicated to Tauscher, and DWM doubtless heavily influenced the decision to rapidly develop a Luger in 9 mm caliber.

Despite the fact that it failed the US Army tests, where it had a clear handicap due to its caliber and being of foreign origin, the Parabellum had a brief commercial success in the United Sates. The popularity that the Luger 1900 model imported by Tauscher had among individuals in the US greatly contributed to building the reputation of the weapon in Europe and to encouraging DWM to continue its dissemination and development. The weapons imported by Tauscher were in all points identical to the models presented for testing, including the marking on the chamber, but they were marked "GERMANY" at the front of the frame, as was required by US regulations for imported weapons.

Luger 1902 model and the American tests

The reticence that many soldiers had in abandoning a revolver with a caliber close to 11 mm for a 7.65 mm semiautomatic had doubtless been detected very early on by George Luger, who worked on developing a larger-caliber cartridge. Starting in 1902, a new version of the Luger appeared chambered for the 9 mm cartridge. The new ammunition was directly extrapolated from the 7.65 mm Parabellum, and the base was kept. The widening of the neck to 9 mm led to the disappearance of the shouldering that gave the 7.65 mm Parabellum its characteristic "bottle" shape.

Luger 1900 "American Eagle" model. The upper part of the safety lever on this example is checkered.

The American eagle, struck on the chamber of Lugers produced for export to the United States, was added from the beginning on the first Luger 1900 sent to the United States, then continued to appear on the chamber of the following models. All types of Luger marked with the American eagle are regrouped by collectors under the name "American Eagle." The magnificent crest on the chamber can be seen here.

This small mark stamped on the interior of the American Eagle Luger frame was at one time considered as a US military marking of the "flaming bomb" type, which is the badge of the ordnance of the US Army. In reality it is a manufacturer's inspection stamp that is found on other Lugers of the first years of production, which were not intended for export to the United States.

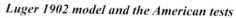

Luger American Eagle model 1902, fitted with a Powell ammunition counter, known as the "1902 Cartridge Counter" by collectors. *Butterfield & Butterfield*

This new ammunition naturally interested the US Army, which made a proposition to Tauscher to select 500 weapons still in perfect condition from the 1,000 "model 1900" Lugers received for the 1902–03 tests in exchange for 500 new Luger pistols in 9 mm caliber. He was also asked to acquire some 25,000 9 mm caliber Luger cartridges.

The new model 1902 Luger pistols, with a 10 cm long barrel, were also struck with the American eagle on the chamber. Their serial numbers went from 22401 to 22450. This batch of weapons was sent to the United Sates by George Luger himself, who arrived in New York in May 1903 on the ocean liner *Kronprinz Wilhelm*.[3]

At the request of the US Army, fifty of these weapons were fitted with a device, designed by the American citizen G. H. Powell, permitting the number of cartridges remaining in the magazine to be checked: the cartridge counter. This device had a special magazine, which is slotted on the left side and fitted with a pin assembled to the magazine floor plate. The left side of the frame, under the grip, is cut out to allow the pin to move fully to the top. In the slotted grip was a scale with gradations in a transparent window where the number of cartridges remaining in the magazine was indicated.

As a result of various tests, the 9 mm caliber still appeared to be insufficient for American soldiers (Colt encountered the same setback with its semiautomatic pistol in .38 caliber). The requests addressed to George Luger to develop a .45-caliber version of his pistol seem to have been denied by him.[4] Three years later, the United States finally adopted the Colt pistol in .45 caliber.

The Lugers used for the military tests were retrieved by the Springfield arsenal, where the ones that were too damaged were destroyed and the others were sold at auction.

The 1906 Model

The failure of Luger in the American army tests did not prevent the company from having a very good commercial career. The improved Luger version, generally known under the name "model 1906," was exported to the US as soon as it appeared on the market in 7.65 mm caliber (with a 12 cm barrel) and in 9 mm caliber (with a 10 cm barrel). These weapons bear the American eagle on the chamber as it appeared on previous versions. Their excellent qualities of robustness and accuracy gave them a commercial success that no other foreign handgun enjoyed in the United States before the end of the Second World War.

3. Michael Reese II, *1900 Luger US Test Trial*, op. cit.
4. Although two examples of the Luger in .45 caliber have been listed.

Two 1902 Lugers. TOP: a standard commercial model; *bottom*: an "American Eagle" with several 9 mm truncated Parabellum cartridges. In the history of weaponry, the 1902 model is above all important for its ammunition: the necessity to propose to the army a caliber superior to the 7.65 mm model 1900 incited DWM to develop this new ammunition, which went on to have an enduring success.

1906 commercial American Eagle no. 28437 with its "Ideal" extendable stock holster

GERMANY marking at the front of the frame on a Luger no. 711v

These Lugers were distributed accompanied by a number of specific accessories such as the Ideal or Behnke-Tiemann stock holster and belt holsters adapted to American tastes.

The 1920 and 1923 models

After World War I, the soldiers of the American Expeditionary Force brought many German military P.08s back home as souvenirs, and this served to reinforce the prestige of the Luger. After Hans Tauscher ceased his professional activity, a new importer, A. F. Stoeger of New York, obtained a virtual monopoly on imports to the United States for the majority of new-production German weapons.[5]

Initially, parts from war surplus were reassembled to produce a great number of Luger variants for the American market. The presentation of these commercial versions, called "model 1920" and "model 1923," is found in volume 1.[6]

At the time when the manufacture of the Luger was transferred from DWM to Mauser, A. F. Stoeger & Co. placed an order for Lugers still marked with the DWM logo, so as not to upset the habits of the American clientele. These weapons, which were delivered in both 7.65 mm and 9 mm Luger, with different barrel lengths,[7] are marked with the American eagle on the chamber and have the following inscriptions on the left side: on the slide, "A. F. STOEGER INC NEW YORK," preceded by "GERMANY." On the frame is "GENUINE LUGER-REGISTERED U.S. PATENT OFFICE." The strong concern to protect the name "LUGER" is explained by the fact that Stoeger had acquired the ownership of this name for the United States.[8]

On the majority of these pistols, the safety zone and the extractor are marked "SAFE" and "LOADED."

Luger "American Eagle" number 411v, made in the 1930s by Mauser for Stoeger, but still bearing a toggle with a DWM marking. Note the magnificent line of this very carefully made piece, in almost perfect condition.

Close-up of the importer's markings stamped on the number 711v. Note the traditional marking "GERMANY" above the ejector.

The beginning of German rearmament in 193 quickly restricted the share of manufacture reserve for export, and so only a few hundred of the Luge Stoegers were delivered. They are therefore highl sought after today by Luger collectors, for thei rarity but also for their remarkable beauty an finish, as are all Lugers made by Mauser befor the war for commercial sale.

The Second World War put an end to thes exports. From 1945 on, the great popularity o the Lugers was continued in the US as America soldiers, having served in Germany, brought bac a great many of the pistols. The importers the took over by buying up old stocks from th Wehrmacht. Then, as has been discussed in th chapter dedicated to Mauser postwar production the Interarms company contacted Mauser durin the 1970s to relaunch production of the Luge. One of the first models was a commemorativ model 70 Parabellum Mauser, with the famou "American Eagle" on the chamber.

5. This monopoly did not apply to surplus or secondhan weapons that other importers such as Pacific Arms o Abercrombie & Fitch commercialized. These surplus weapor did not have the American eagle on the chamber.
6. Luc Guillou, *The Luger P.08, Vol. 1: The First World Wa and Weimar Years*.
7. It was also possible for American buyers to order one o these pistols accompanied by a barrel-slide assembl interchangeable with barrels of different lengths.
8. After the war, Stoeger had the pistol .22LR made in th United States, whose external appearance resembled that o the Parabellum, but whose mechanism was completely differen This weapon was sold quite legally under the name "Luger, since Stoeger owned the rights in the United States.

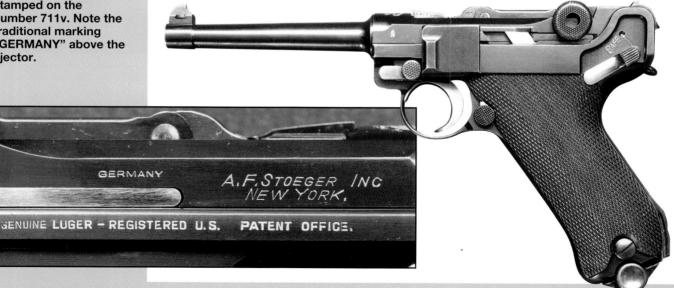

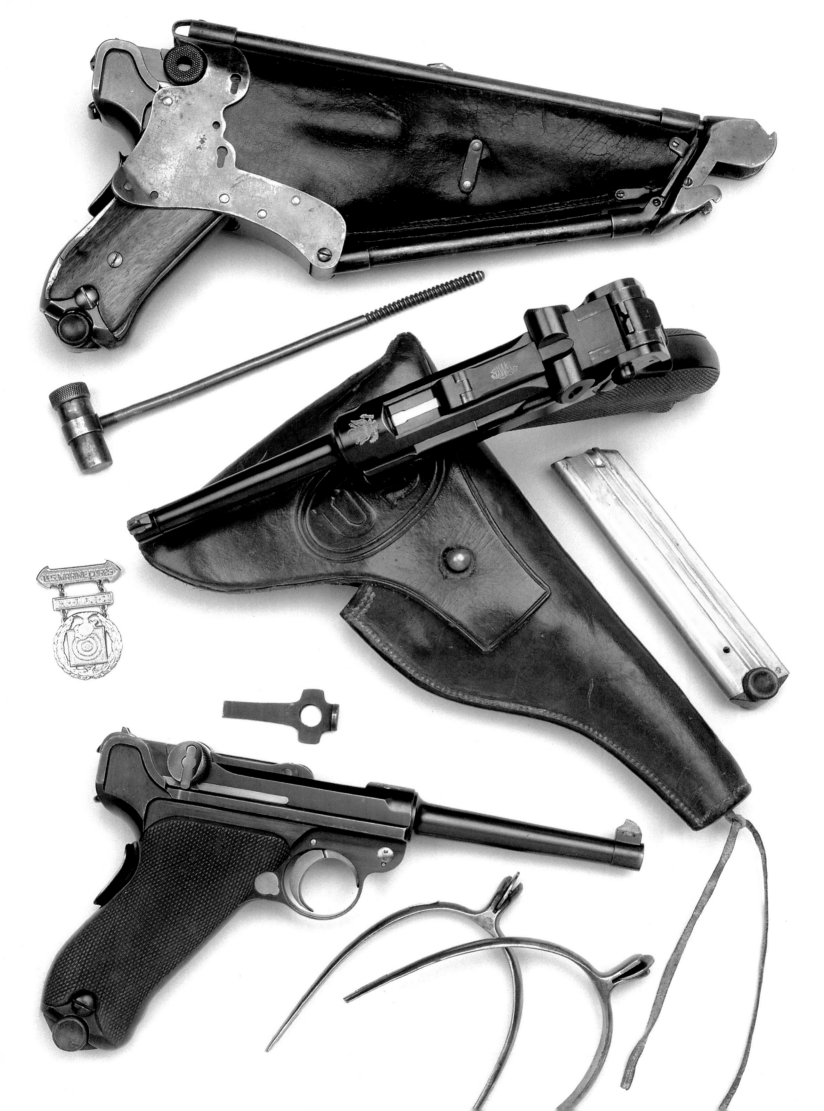

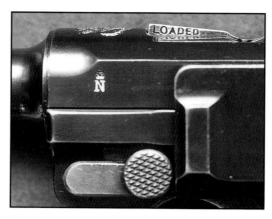

Marking in English on the extractor. Note the presence of the American eagle on the chamber and the vertical crowned "N" mark on the slide and bolt head. These parts were retrieved by Mauser from DWM. Mauser, on the other hand, assembled a new barrel in 7.65 mm caliber, marked with its own proof mark, "U" with double crown (perhaps even Mauser replaced a 9 mm DWM barrel already mounted on its weapon by one of its own barrels in 7.65 mm to meet Stoeger's demand).

"Safe" marking in the safety zone

Still today, the reproductions of the Luger, such as those proposed by the Mitchell company, have kept the tradition of stamping the prestigious "American Eagle" on the chamber.

THE DUTCH LUGER

From the first years of the twentieth century, the Dutch army started testing different automatic pistols: Mannlicher, Bergmann, Mauser model 1896, and Parabellum.

At the end of this series of tests, the Luger was not adopted by the metropolitan troops of the land army, since they preferred the Browning 10/22, but it became regulation in the colonial forces stationed in the Dutch Indies from 1911 onward, and then in the navy.

Several beautiful Dutch Lugers, *from top to bottom*: a DWM 1906 model, no. 1077; an example used by the Dutch air force, no. 10783; a 1923 naval model, no. 1060; an example made for the colonial forces by Vickers Ltd., no. 7780. Even though similar to the rod used by the Dutch army, the one in this photo is a Portuguese rod with a notched end (Dutch rods have a smooth end with a single slot for a flannelette to pass through).

The 1911 model (*"Pistool M 11"*)

From a mechanical point of view, this was a 1906 model with a 10 cm barrel, chambered in 9 mm Para, made by DWM. The principal distinctive elements of this model were the following:

- commercial numbering on the weapon; magazine not numbered

- the marking "Rust" accompanied by an arrow, indicating the safety position on the safety lever

- the marking "Geladen" ("loaded") stamped on both sides of the extractor

- Dutch proof mark, representing a crowned "W," on the right side of the receiver on the first deliveries, then later on the left side

- sometimes the presence of small figures stamped on the barrel, corresponding to the date the barrel was changed

- common but not exclusive presence of a brass plate, welded under the left handgrip or at the front of the trigger guard, with a stamp of the abbreviations indicating the unit where the weapon was assigned

Dutch proof mark "W" crowned (Queen Wilhelmina)

Luger M11 no. 10783 of the Dutch colonial forces, with its regulation pouch and accessories

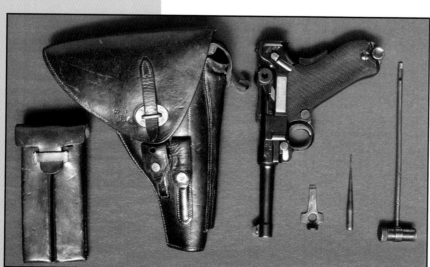

A lot of Dutch Lugers have a brass plate with the marking of the unit to which the weapon was assigned. Here we see the plate welded on the left side of the frame of a Luger assigned to the health department based in the hospital at Weltewreden in the Dutch East Indies.

Example of a regimental plate, here soldered to the trigger guard. The initials SW ("Stijders Wielrijders") are those of a combat cyclist unit; 452 is the number of the unit. Note the British stamp at the forward of the frame.

Three Dutch Lugers with accessories, *from top to bottom*: model made between the wars by DWM/BKIW for the navy, no. 1060; another naval model made by Mauser in 1939, (N)2640v); an example, destined for colonial troops, with toggle marked "VICKERS," serial no. 7780

The number of model 1911 pistols delivered by DWM before the beginning of the First World War is estimated to be 4,181. Mobilization suspended a new Dutch order of 400 weapons and put an end to any new delivery coming from Germany until 1921.

The "*Vickers*"-marked Lugers

From the beginning of the century in Europe, the giants of the armaments industry—DWM in Germany, the Steyr factory in Austria, the national war arms factory in Belgium, and Vickers Ltd. in Great Britain—were closely linked by a set of mutual-equity shares. The clauses of the Treaty of Versailles forbade the production and export of weapons of war, but just after the First World War, the DWM establishment came up with a ploy enabling them to satisfy new and pressing requests for Lugers from Dutch colonial forces. Relying on the fact that the export of spare parts and unfinished weapons did not fall under the prohibitions of the Treaty of Versailles, DWM exported the necessary components to Great Britain for the assembly of the Lugers ordered by The Netherlands. Between 1921 and 1928 these parts were assembled, tested, and marked by Vickers, which then reexported around 6,000 semifinished pistols to the Bandung arsenal (Java) in the Dutch Indies, where they received their final finishing (bluing) and grip plates, made at the armorers' school attached to that arsenal. These weapons principally differ from the 1911 models described earlier by the following features:

- the marking "VICKERS LTD" stamped on the central part of the toggle

- the locally made plates, with a cruder checkering than on the DWM and marked "GS" (for Geweermakers School) on the inside

Interior of the grips of a Vickers Luger: the marking "GS," which can be seen in an oval, is that of the Geweermakers School (Gunsmiths' School) of the Bantung arsenal in the Dutch Indies, which undertook the final finish of the Vickers Lugers. The number refers to the weapon number.

LEFT: safety marking on a Vickers Luger (1906-type safety)

RIGHT: safety marking (1908-type safety) on a Luger of the Royal Dutch Navy

Marking on a Mauser P.08 made in 1940 for the Dutch navy. Due to the declaration of war, these pistols were requisitioned for the Wehrmacht and not delivered to the Netherlands.

German military stamp on a 1940 Dutch Mauser Banner (although this pistol was originally a commercial-type production)

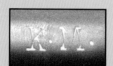

"KM" marking (Koninklijke Marine) on the grip of a DWM Luger

- the presence of British test stamps on the barrel, toggle, and frame

Second delivery of DWM Parabellum to Dutch colonial forces

Starting in 1927, with the relaxation of the application of clauses of the Treaty of Versailles, DWM was able to supply Parabellums directly to the Netherlands.

Between 1928 and 1937, 3,839 of these weapons were delivered to the colonial forces. These Lugers are mechanically identical to the 1911 models but differ in the following points:

- simplification in the machining of the frame, put into effect during the First World War, and a slight increase in the thickness of the metal in the rear part of the frame

- commercial-type numbering with five, rather than four, figures; German commercial stamp (vertical crowned "N") on the right side of the receiver

- marking composed of a "K" and "L" in a circle, whose meaning remains open to interpretation, stamped on the right side of the receiver

DWM/BKIW delivery for the Royal Navy

Between 1928 and 1936, 2,129 other Lugers were delivered to the Royal Dutch Navy. This period was notable for DWM abandoning the production of Lugers for the benefit of Mauser.

The Lugers delivered to the navy were probably assembled by Mauser from the remainder of DWM parts. They still had the DWM monogram on the toggle. These pistols are no longer 1906 models as were the previous ones, but 1908 models without a safety lock and fitted with a stock lug at the base of the grip. The direction of the safety is consequently reversed in relation to the previous models. They are also distinct from the models sent to colonial troops on the following points:

- commercial numbering with four figures

- absence of the "KL" or "KOL" stamp

- occasional presence of the initials "KM" (for "Koninklijke Marine" Royal Navy)

The examples made by Mauser are identifiable by the test stamp of "U" with double crown replacing the "N"-crowned stamp.

Mauser delivery for the Royal Navy

Between 1937 and 1940, the Dutch navy ordered a final series of P.08s from Mauser: 200 in 1937, 100 in 1938, and 225 in 1939. These weapons are the commercial Mauser type identifiable by the "Mauser Banner" logo struck on the toggle and the test stamp of "U" with double crown. The four-figure numbering is military type. The 1938 and 1939 specimens have a serial number followed by the letter "v" (as indeed were the majority of Mauser-made P.08s for export at this period).

A last delivery of 600 weapons (numbered from 2655v to 3254v), planned for 1940, was impounded due to the state of war between the Netherlands and Germany. This batch was given to German forces after the Waffenamt inspection stamps had been put on the right side of the receiver and on the barrel.

THE PORTUGUESE LUGER

Confronted with the necessity of protecting the distant colonies in Africa and Asia, Portugal had made a significant effort to modernize its weapons from the end of the nineteenth century. The adoption of a Guesdes small-caliber shotgun with a Kropathchek system in 1886 was followed in 1904 by a Mauser rifle with a bolt mechanism modified by Col. Vergueiro.

In 1908, the Portuguese army, which had started to evaluate Luger pistols around 1900, adopted a weapon of this type called m/908. This opened the way for numerous other orders, which continued until 1943.

This Luger is characterized by the following markings:

- the monogram crowned "M2" on the chamber, which signifies that the weapon was adopted under the reign of King Manuel II

- the extractor is marked "CARREGADA" on the left side

- the presence of a tax mark, representing an equilateral triangle in a circle, on the left of the slide, on the rear of the frame, and at the base of the magazine

- a commercial-type numbering probably extending from 1 to 5000; such is the estimation of the importance of the first Portuguese order (3,500 or 5,000 weapons, depending on the author)

After the revolution of 1910, which removed Manuel II from power and established a republic in Portugal, the monograms M2 (or at least the crowns) on some Lugers were filed off by concerned owners who wished to show their allegiance to the new regime.

The model 1910 Luger of the Royal Portuguese Navy

The Portuguese navy adopted the Luger pistol two years after the army, and the weapon entered service in 1910 under the name "Pistola Luger Parabellum Marinha Portuguesa 1910," or abbreviated to "m/910." The contract for the supply of 350 weapons to be delivered within three months was signed on November 23, 1909, between the Portuguese Purchasing Commission and DWM.

The Luger pistols that were still found in the arsenals of the Portuguese army at the beginning of the 1960s were bought by American importers. These buyers also managed to acquire certain official archives relative to these weapons, a highly rare occurrence in the weapons trade. Because of this, we can now benefit from the quite-detailed knowledge of the use of the Luger pistol in Portugal.

This section of the book on the Portuguese Lugers contains information collected during the examination of this archive, as well as the Portuguese Lugers themselves upon their arrival in the United States by American collectors such as Luger specialist Charles Kenyon.

The model 1908 Luger with "M2" monogram
Despite its adoption by Portugal in 1908, this pistol in fact was a Luger 1906 type with a short frame and a 12 cm barrel chambered in 7.65 mm Parabellum. Its regulation name is "m/908."

Portuguese colonial forces using a Maxim machine gun on a mount. The chief (*standing on the right*) has a holster for two spare Luger magazines.

"M2" chamber monogram

CARREGADA marking on the extractor of an m/908

Luger m/908 placed on a box for two spare magazines

Inspection stamp (equilateral triangle in a circle, which is found on the slide, the rear of the frame, and the magazine bottom on the Luger M2)

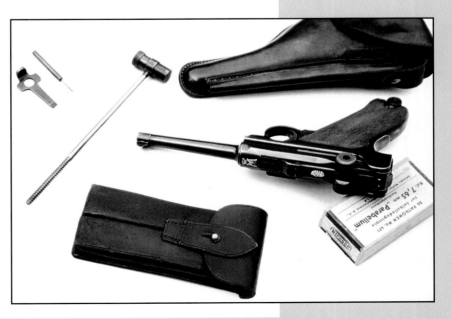

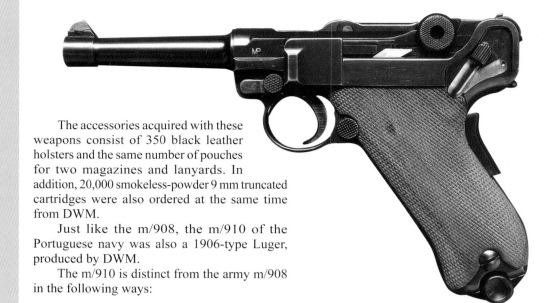

The accessories acquired with these weapons consist of 350 black leather holsters and the same number of pouches for two magazines and lanyards. In addition, 20,000 smokeless-powder 9 mm truncated cartridges were also ordered at the same time from DWM.

Just like the m/908, the m/910 of the Portuguese navy was also a 1906-type Luger, produced by DWM.

The m/910 is distinct from the army m/908 in the following ways:

- its caliber: 9 mm Parabellum instead of 7.65 mm Parabellum

- the length of its barrel: 10 cm instead of 12 cm

- its markings on the chamber: a naval anchor with a crown above (in the first delivery)

- the "MP" proof mark on the left side of the chamber (instead of the equilateral triangle in a circle that is found in this position and on various others on the m/908)

As on the m/908, the m/910 has "CARREGADA" ("loaded" in Portuguese) stamped on the left side of the extractor. These weapons are numbered in the commercial style, with numbers from one to four figures. It is likely that the numbering was not continuous.

It seems that the first delivery of these weapons took place in the spring of 1910. The number of weapons sent to Portugal on this occasion is not known, but if the numbering is taken into account, then the amount was very low: several hundred, and in any case most certainly fewer than one thousand pistols.

The model 1910 Luger of the Republican Navy

In 1910 Portugal underwent a regime crisis that culminated in King Manoel II being exiled at the end of the summer and the proclamation of the republic taking place on October 5, 1910.

It was therefore asked of DWM to stamp the letters "RP" above the anchor (for "Republica Portuguesa") rather than a crown on the chamber of those pistols still to be delivered.

The inspection mark "MP" appearing on the models with a crowned anchor on the right side of the slide principally no longer appeared on the models with the "RP" monogram. This marking is either totally absent or replaced by the "RP" marking.

Apart from these particularities concerning the markings, these pistols are totally identical to the previous ones. Some slides of this series with the same MP initials struck on the left side as the royal navy models can be encountered.

Information concerning the number of Lugers produced with the RP marking and their numbering differs depending on the author; the only official document that was found reports a delivery of 150 weapons numbered from 501 to 650 in July 1912, and alludes to a previous delivery.

American historian Charles Kenyon was able to examine specimens from the serial numbers in the 352 to 639 section.

If it is accepted that the numbering of the Lugers with Republican Navy marking started at number 1 and that it was continuous over the two deliveries that seemed to have taken place, the number of these weapons is around 650. In fact, on the basis of the study of numbers listed today, collectors consider that the numbering of this series probably did not begin at number 1 and that hardly more than three or four hundred Lugers with "RP" markings were delivered by DWM. To date, they were identical to the m/908, but slightly shorter.

The marking on the magazine used with the navy models remains open to discussion: some markings "Cal.9M/M" in cursive script have been observed on the magazine bottom found in these weapons, as have markings representing the triangle in a circle that is a common feature of the m/908. Bearing in mind the interchangeability between the m/908 and m/910 magazines, it is likely that army pistol magazines were inserted in a naval Luger at some point.

The Luger of the National Republican Guard (GNR)

This is a small batch of 564 weapons that were delivered to the Guardia Nacional Republicana (National Republican Guard), abbreviated to "GNR."

The number of these weapons is known exactly, since the Portuguese archives concerning the conclusion of the contract remain intact today. The same source allows us to know that these weapons were delivered in September 1935, accompanied by a consignment of ammunition specially made by the Austrian cartridge factory Hirtenberger.

This Luger, called "Pistola Parabellum da Guardia Nacional Republicana" in Portugal, is chambered in 7.65 mm caliber Parabellum. It has a short frame, a 12 cm barrel, and a safety lock, but without a stock lug. Its nickeled magazine and aluminum bottom are without marking. The "GNR" Lugers also present the following particularities:

- presence of a stylized GNR monogram on the chamber

- central portion of the toggle marked with a small Mauser logo

- serial numbers from 1921v to 2484v included

- markings in Portuguese of "CARREGADA" on the extractor and "SEGURANCA" on the safety zone

These weapons were worn in a black leather holster similar to that of the m/908 but were equipped with two slings, allowing it to be worn at a lower level. This holster had a pouch under the flap for a

takedown and loading tool (without any particular marking) and two pouches on the right side: one for a cleaning rod (principally with a cylindrical metal handle acting as a lubrication tin and a rod with a helical contoured surface for attaching cleaning cloths) and the other for a pin remover.

A magazine pouch with two compartments was also assigned to every holder of a Luger. The pouches that we have been able to examine have a crudely stamped "GNR" with the date "1935" on the back. Such markings can also be seen on the back of the holster.

Type P.08 Portuguese Luger

In a communication published in the March 1996 edition of *Gun Report* (vol. 42, no. 4), Charles Kenyon listed the orders that Portugal made to Mauser following on from the "GNR" series:

- September 1935: A small batch of pistols (considered to be from 70 to 80) identical to the model delivered to the National Republican Guard (GNR) but with a 10 cm barrel in 9 mm caliber Parabellum and without markings on the chamber. The serial numbers of these weapons most likely ranged from 2483v to 2555v.

- June 1937: a possible fifty further specimens (thirty-eight examined), identical to the model described above, with numbers between 4301v to 4350v

Afterward, pistols without a thumb safety but equipped with a lug at the bottom of the buttstock and with a frame reinforced at the rear started to be delivered, meaning that apart from

Marking in the safety zone

Close-up of the Mauser test stamp used on commercial weapons until the beginning of the war, before being replaced by the eagle with wings spread above the letter "N"

"GNR" monogram on the chamber and small Mauser logo on the toggle

GNR Luger serial no. 2362. Apart from its chamber marking, the weapon differs from the m/908 in the following points: the presence of a crowned "U" test stamp on the left side of the slide, the "SEGURANCA" marking in the safety zone, the shorter trigger bar (type "n/A"), the grips with finer checkering than those of the m/908 with "M2" marking, and the magazine with aluminum bottom. The pistol here is placed on a Portuguese holster in tawny leather normally delivered with Lugers produced later than the GNR, but shaped to house all Luger models (with a 10 or 12 cm barrel) used in Portugal.

certain details in the markings, these pistols are identical to the German P.08:

- November 1940: seventeen specimens with numbers from 6942v and 6972v, with a safety zone marked "SEGUR-ANCA" and the extractor "CARRE-GADA"; the toggle has a large Mauser Banner rather than a small one as on previous versions; the chamber is marked 41.

- October 1941: Thirty pistols possibly destined for the navy, numbered from 6951v to 6980w, with markings identical to those described previously. This consignment seems to have three training models numbered 27, 28, and 29.

- 1942: Twenty-four pistols identical to the previous ones but with a safety zone marked "GESICHERT" and "GELADEN" on the extractor and "42" on the chamber. These weapons are numbered from 8024 y (or 8026 y?) to 8050 y.

- February 1943: A final series of P.08s, identical to the previous one but with the toggle marked "byf." The numbering of examples of this type examined by Charles Kenyon ranged from 137 m to 9416 m.

The last order of the P.08 was probably made by Portugal to Mauser in February 1943. It is estimated to be slightly more than 4,500 pistols (possibly 4,578, numbered from 865 to 5263).

Portuguese Lugers, *from top to bottom*: an m/908 with "M2" chamber marking and a GNR Luger positioned on a GNR holster; an m/910 of the Republican Navy (placed on a leather lanyard for Luger), of the type used by Portugal; an m/943 placed on its regulation holster

These weapons were held in a specific holster, with a housing for a takedown tool under a large flap and another housing for a steel cleaning rod (of the type often referred to by collectors as "sardine tin key"). A braided leather strap completed the ensemble.

Portugal was doubtless the last country in the world to purchase Luger pistols. From the end of the 1940s onward, these weapons started to be replaced by the Walther P.38, then by the Browning GP 35.

The Luger nonetheless remained in service for many years, and some were still being used in the 1970s during operations in Angola and Mozambique.

Portugal was very faithful to the Luger pistol. FROM LEFT TO RIGHT: an example marked with the "M2" monogram of King Manuel II, adopted in 1908; a naval model adopted in 1910 (here the variant has the marking of the navy of the Portuguese republic); an example delivered in 1935 to the Republican National Guard; and a P.08 Mauser of the last delivery carried out in 1943

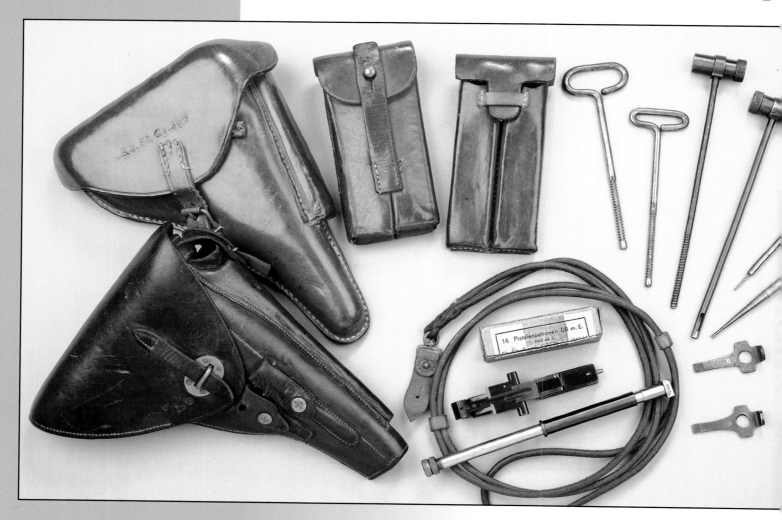

Several examples of accessories of various origins, all in superb condition, are presented here. FROM LEFT TO RIGHT: a Dutch holster; a German holster marked Kü.Flo.Gr. 306; an Iranian magazine pouch; a Dutch pouch; various rods: a large-handle model, a narrow-handle model, an all-steel Portuguese type, a Dutch type (identifiable by the slot machined at the base of the stem for storing a cloth); a German pin remover; a Dutch pin remover; two stripping tools; and, in the center, a rolled Portuguese lanyard, a .22-caliber conversion kit, and a box of cartridges.

**Marking done by hand:
Kü.Flo.Gr. 306
(KÜSTENFLIEGER
GRUPPE 306)**

Less costly than the weapons themselves and able to be purchased and owned without being subject to regulations, Luger accessories are increasingly sought after by collectors. As a complement to the mainly German accessories of the 1900–1933 period presented in volume 1, and those appearing throughout all chapters of both volumes, we have chosen to group together various post-1933 Luger accessories from Germany and other countries in a single chapter in this volume.

HOLSTERS
GERMAN HOLSTERS
Military-type holsters

These holsters are very close to those of the First World War (fastened by a slanted leather tab sewn to the flap, fixed on a buckle on the left side of the holster, magazine pouch on the right side, pouch for takedown tool under the flap). The identity of the manufacturer appears initially in full, with the complete date of manufacture (in four figures). The stamp of the inspection office of the Waffenamt, who verified the conformity of the holsters upon delivery to the Wehrmacht, was struck next to these markings.

The lettering of these stamps evolved over time (eagle with lowered wings at the beginning of the war, followed by a very simplified design with vertical wings). These indications are usually stamped at the rear of the holster or sometimes at the front of certain early-production models.

Considering the large number of weapons in service, the army demanded that the type of weapon to which they corresponded should be marked on the holsters and sometimes also on the magazines, as here: "P.08." This provision strengthened during the war but was however sometimes forgotten by some manufacturers.

The type of weapon the holster was destined for (P.08 in this case) started to be indicated on the back of the holster during the war.

During the war, the clear identity of the manufacturer was replaced by a code generally composed of three letters.

The date appears either in full or just the last two figures of the year are mentioned. These holsters were used by the three components of the armed forces (Wehrmacht): Heer (army), Kriegsmarine (navy), and Luftwaffe (air force),

Heavy-bomber crews attend a briefing before leaving on a mission. Each man is wearing a P.08 holster on his regulation belt. *ECPA*

Type of holster used by the German army during the Second World War

Marking on the front side of the holster: "LEDERWERKE KARL ACKVA / BAD KREUZNACH 1934"

Marking of the AUWAERTER & BUBECK A.G. firm of Stuttgart on a military holster of 1935

Military holster made by FR&K VOGELS of Köln Deutz in 1936. Note the stamp typical of this period (eagle with lowered wings) of the WaffenAmt 387.

Gustav Rheinhardt, used by the navy during the last years of the Weimar Republic or the first years of the Third Reich

Holster for P.08s of the Kriegsmarine, with the marking "MORDHORST KIEL"

E. LÜNEN-SCHLOSS SOLINGEN production of Solingen in 1939. A marking with three stems above the Waffenamt stamp could indicate the utilization by an SS unit, but this type of symbol should be considered with caution; their appearance on leather equipment was not regulation, and also the ease with which they can be forged should be taken into account.

C. Otto GEHRCKENS-PINNEBERG 1940

Marking "fuq 1942" on a Kriegsmarine holster. This code is that of the saddler COTTBUSER LEDERWARENWERK CURT VOGEL.

Gunners of a SS police unit (Ordnungspolizei), positioned with their MG08 machine gun on the rooftops of Warsaw in 1939. All three men are wearing a police holster for a P.08 at their belt.

Police holsters

A feature of these holsters is that they are fastened by a vertical tab with a button fastening on a flap. These are found in different tints from light brown to black, depending on the equipment worn by the police units to which they were assigned.

The identity of the manufacturer and the date of production most often appears on the back of the holster, along with police inspection stamps (police eagle). Many holsters dating from the Weimar Republic continued to be worn under the Third Reich by members of the police (these holsters are generally marked with the initial of the inspector, surrounded by rays or the initials "TP"). In some cases these unit markings appear on the back of the holster. This practice was abandoned under the Third Reich, and certain other older markings were stamped over.

These holsters were used by law enforcement operating in Germany and in occupied territories, by certain border units, and by police regiments operating at the front (including the SS Polizei Division).

but also by the majority of units of the Waffen-SS, with the exception of units making up the police regiments, which kept the police-type holsters.

These holsters were generally made with cow leather dyed black. They can be found in natural leather, or in leather dyed brown (in particular for certain holsters used by the Luftwaffe). Some pigskin leather holsters were also used.

Weimar police inspection stamp (initial of the inspector surrounded by rays) on a holster of the Weimar police made by Schambach & Co., 1929

ROBERT LARSEN 1933 marking

Schambach Berlin 1941 police holster. Note the reception eagle of the police.

"TP" police marking on the reverse of a Robert Larsen Berlin 1935 holster

Unidentified marking on the inside of a police holster

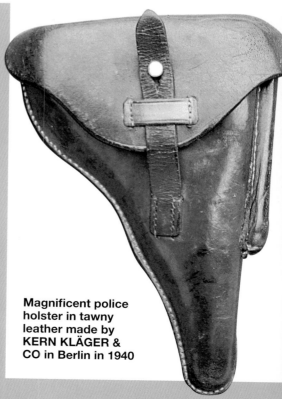

Magnificent police holster in tawny leather made by KERN KLÄGER & CO in Berlin in 1940

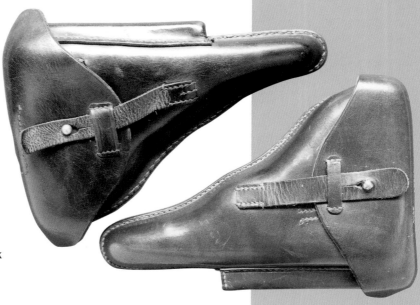

Two magnificent German commercial holsters made on the eve of the Second World War. These holsters are fastened by a vertical tab reminiscent of the police holsters. A black holster made by Wunderlich Berlin in 1936, a tawny holster made by Akah (commercial name of the Albrecht Kind firm).

Markings stamped on the back of these two holsters

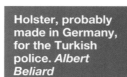

Holster, probably made in Germany, for the Turkish police. *Albert Beliard*

WISS HOLSTERS

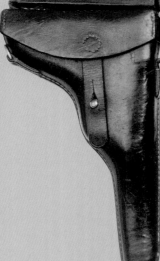
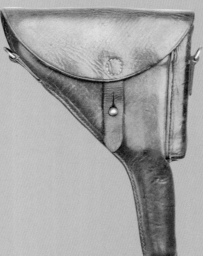

Three variants of Swiss military holsters: the two models on the left are for 1900 and 1900/06 models, and the one on the right for the 06/29. *Marc de Fromont*

Marking on a military holster made by Glauser in Berne in 1917

Inspection stamp under the flap on a holster on a Swiss military holster

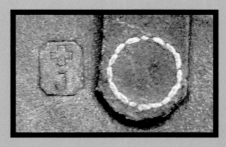

Marking of the manufacturer E. TINGUELY of Alterswil (date of production 1941)

Swiss NCOs practicing firing with the Parabellum between the wars. *Maurice Sublet*

Several Swiss commercial holsters. These were heavily influenced by military models. *Marc de Fromont*

Marking on the strap of a Swiss commercial holster

Swiss accessories pouch

AMERICAN HOLSTERS

Holster and magazine pouch made for commercial sale in the United States by H. H. Heiser of Denver, Colorado

US holster for a Luger

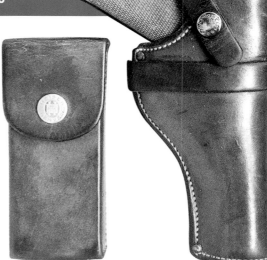

Markings appearing on the back of the Heiser holster and pouch

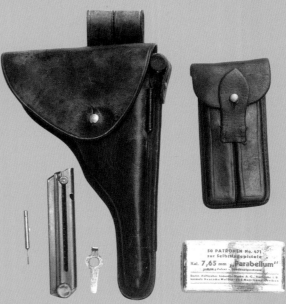

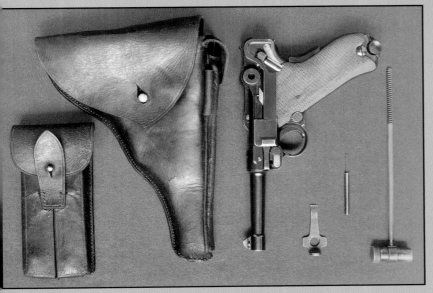

Accessories for the Portuguese naval model 1910 Luger

Magazine pouch and holster destined for the Luger of the National Republican Guard

SWEDEN

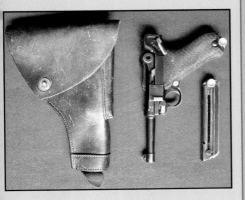

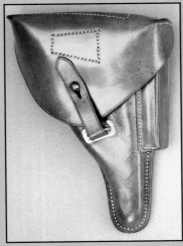

Holster for P.08 Mausers delivered to Portugal

Mauser-produced Luger, serial no. 7629 w, delivered to Sweden for tests around 1934, accompanied by a Swedish-made holster and its spare magazine

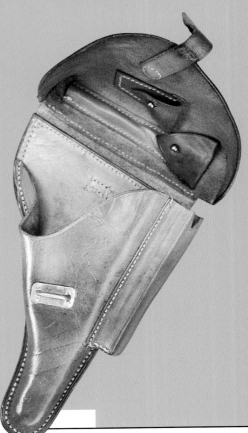

BULGARIA

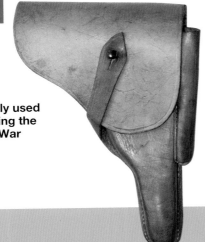

Holster probably used in Bulgaria during the Second World War

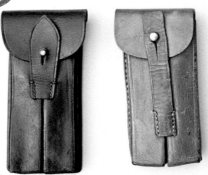

LEFT: Portuguese pouch for two spare magazines, marked on the reverse: "A.E." (Arsenal de Ejercito). RIGHT: Iranian magazine pouch.

Holster used by the
Vopo for the P.08 pistols.
Wolfgang Kroker

German holster modified
after the war by the
addition of a hook to be
worn on a US-type belt.
This type of modification
is encountered on
holsters having been in
service in the Danish
and Norwegian armies,
among others.

OTHER POST-1945 COMMERCIAL HOLSTERS

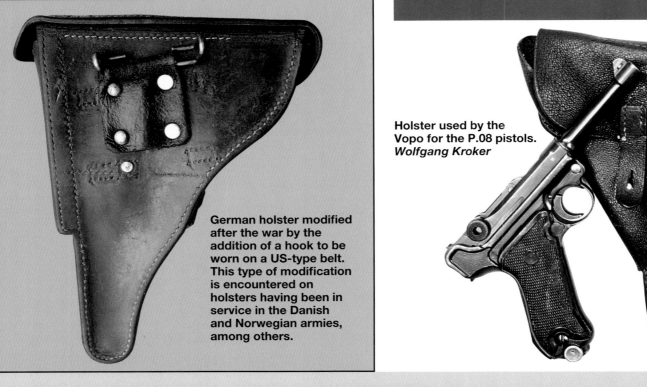

Marking on a
"Gil" holster for
Luger pistols

Two very fine holsters in
molded leather for Luger
with 10 cm and 15 cm
barrels made in France
by the GIL firm in the
1960s. This company
stopped making holsters
for handguns a few
years ago. These
high-quality holsters,
made from oak-bark
tanned leather and very
stylish, are rapidly
becoming very
collectible.

Marking on a
Bauer Bros. holster

Marking on an AKAH shoulder
holster. Note that this firm
kept its prewar logo.

Open holster in
tan leather made
in the United States
by Bauer Bros.

AKAH postwar shoulder
holster in natural leather
and a Lebanese-made
holster in green canvas

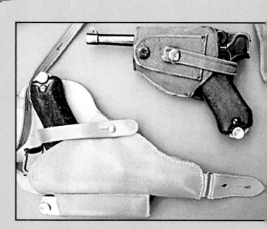

MAGAZINES

While the majority of weapons makers continued using clips for automatic pistols with fixed magazines, starting in 1893 Hugo Borchardt opted for a pistol with a removable magazine. If the choice seems obvious today, it was less so at that time: the removable magazine was fragile, heavy, and, above all, costly. In his book *Die Pistole 08*, Joachim Görtz points out that at the beginning of the century, the price of a Luger magazine was twenty-five times that of a clip for a Mauser C.96.

From 1900 to today, a large variety of magazines were conceived for the Luger pistol. The drum magazines (*Trommelmagazin*), destined for the long Luger, were presented in volume 1.

1900–1923: MAGAZINE WITH BODY IN TWO PARTS AND WOODEN BOTTOM

Basic model

Directly inspired from those of the Borchardt pistol, the first magazines of Parabellum model 1900 are composed of the following:

- A body made from two half shells in 0.5 mm thick sheet metal. These parts, constituting the rear and front parts of the magazine, were folded, interlocked, then crimped. A noteworthy improvement was brought to these magazines, compared to the Borchardt pistol, by the addition of a guideway allowing a knob solid with the magazine follower to move. On the other hand, the body of the magazine obtained by this method had a certain fragility that could engender deformations likely to cause errors in the feeding of the pistol.

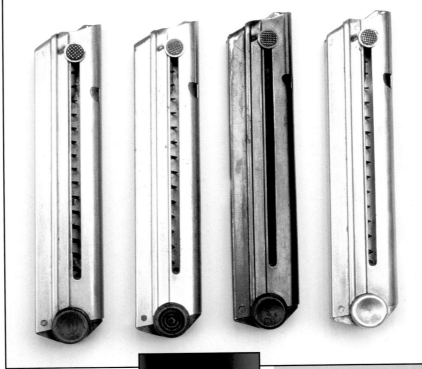

Magazine with wooden bottom stamped with the initials "GL." These initials are found on some early-made Lugers. The hypothesis that prevails is that these letters represent the initials of George Luger.

Some examples of magazines with a body in two parts, FROM LEFT TO RIGHT: magazine with nickel-plated body and wooden bottom, naval variant, wooden base mount on a bronze body, aluminum bottom, nickel-plated body. *Marc de Fromont*

Magazine marked "Caliber 9m/m," seen more often on 1902 and 1906 Lugers in this caliber

Magazine bottom in wood, nonmarked for commercial Lugers or some military export contracts (from 1900 to around 1923–25)

Magazine bottom in wood for the German military P.08 produced by DWM, 1908–11 period

Magazine bottom in wood for the DWM military P.08, as it appeared from 1912

Unit marking (probably the police of the Weimar Republic) at the rear of the magazine bottom in wood

Magazine for Erfurt P.08 with two inspection stamps, bearing the serial number "992b." Type of marking stamped between 1912 and 1914.

Spare magazine for the same weapon, identifiable by the "+" marking. This magazine was housed principally in the holster transport pouch.

Magazine for Erfurt P.08 with a single inspection stamp (1914–18 period)

Magazine with wood bottom for a Luger of the Weimar police

Large number and stamp of the German Imperial Navy (crowned "M")

- A steel magazine follower, with a knob on the right side. This knob facilitates the loading of the magazine with the help of the thumb, or the movement of the magazine follower downward with the help of a special tool. In addition, after the last cartridge is fired, this knob positions itself under the magazine catch, which it then pushes upward during the opening of the toggle, in order to prevent it from closing.

- A bottom in wood, having a cylindrical part with convex extremities, designed to facilitate the handling of the magazine. This bottom slotted into the lower part of the magazine in which it is held by a small pin. On some magazines, such as those in the Lugers delivered to Switzerland, the cylindrical portion of the bottom in wood is reinforced in the center by a metal cylinder,

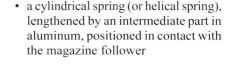

- a cylindrical spring (or helical spring), lengthened by an intermediate part in aluminum, positioned in contact with the magazine follower

Very soon after the Luger entered service the thickness of the loading knob was slightly increased so as to improve handling and doubtless also to increase its reach on the slide stop, holding it open after the firing of the last cartridge. The depth of the guideway, milled in the grip of the pistol to allow the loading knob to move, was increased as a consequence. The dimensions of the knob and guideway subsequently remained unchanged. The first model 1900 Lugers with a flat loading knob are extremely rare today.

Some magazine bottoms of the Lugers 1900 and 1906 are fitted with a metal reinforcement positioned in the center of their cylindrical part. This is particularly the case for magazines destined for Swiss Luger models 1900 and 1900/06.

This first variation of magazines with wood bottom continued to be produced both for civilian and military weapons of 7.65 mm or 9 mm caliber until just after the First World War. On the first Luger 1900 magazines, the polish of the magazine frame is rougher than on later ones. Some traces, parallel to the magazine follower spring pin, are visible under the nickel plating on the body of the magazine, giving a slightly more matte appearance with a white sheen. The later examples are perfectly polished, and in new condition, no trace is visible on the body of the magazine. The nickel plate appearance has more of a satin finish with a yellow sheen.

Magazine with wood bottom for Luger of the Portuguese contract, marked with an equilateral triangle in a circle

Magazine with wood bottom produced by "Fabrique Federale d'armes" of Berne for the Swiss Luger 1900/06

Magazine for Dutch Luger, identifiable by the small clamping spring positioned at the rear of the base

VARIANTS

Magazine for cartridge counter system

When the American army tried the Luger 1902 model, fifty-five examples were fitted with a cartridge counter device attributable to an American citizen, G. H. Powell, which allowed the shooter to check the contents of the magazine at any moment. The Powell cartridge counter has a window cut in the right grip of the weapon; this window is covered with a transparent material marked with the numbers 1 to 7. As each round was fired, the indicator would advance, with the follower showing how many rounds were left in the pistol's magazine. The magazines modified to be used with the Powell cartridge counter have a window on the left side, in which a pointer solid with the follower moved.

Navy

In adopting the Luger 1904 model, the German Imperial Navy chose to fit it with a magazine with a bottom machined with concentric circles, probably designed to improve grip. This variant of magazine seems to have been used only on naval Lugers. The relief of concentric circles was to be abandoned on naval Lugers during the First World War. The examples used from then on by the navy were distinct from the other models by the markings on the base.

Dutch

The wood-bottom magazines used by the Dutch army were fitted with a flat spring designed to reinforce the fixing of the base in the magazine body. This part is positioned at the rear part of the base and locks in a slot cut in the rear part of the magazine frame.

Magazines with aluminum bottom

From 1925 on, the German army (the Reichswehr) chose to abandon the wooden bottom, considered too sensitive both to impact and dampness, in favor of an aluminum bottom, considered to be more robust. The transition between the two types of bases took place gradually, as stocks were used up. The Luger sold in the civilian sector often continued to have wood-bottom magazines until the 1930s.

The protection of the magazine body by a nickel plate, judged to be too expensive, was abandoned around 1936 in favor a single immersion bluing, giving a glossy-black appearance to this part. It should be noted that the nickel plating of the last magazines with aluminum bottom is whiter than on earlier examples, which could suggest a slight modification of the alloy composition used to make the protection of the body.

Haenel magazines

A new, more robust type of magazine appeared near the end of the 1930s, often called "milled magazine," and was made by the Haenel firm and based on a principle developed by the brothers Hugo and Hans Schmeisser. The body of this magazine was made from long sections of 1.5 mm

Magazines with aluminum bottom for P.08s made by the firm Simson & Co. of Suhl, for the Reichswehr between 1925 and 1933–34. The weapons and accessories produced at this period by this producer for the Reichswehr have inspection stamps representing an eagle above a figure "6" (referred to as "eagle/6" by collectors).

Unidentified stamp (although probably belonging to the police)

Uncommon variant of the Simson stamp: the letter "S" in a triangle, then in a circle. The figure "1" may indicate that this is a police magazine.

Unmarked aluminum-bottom magazine for commercial Lugers made from 1923 to the Second World War

Aluminum bottom marked "7,65" for a commercial Luger or an unidentified military export contract

Aluminum bottom marked "GERMANY" on a commercial magazine destined for export

Simson production for the Weimar navy; the letter "N" indicates its use by the North Sea naval base.

Police Luger magazine of the Weimar period. The figure "1" indicates that this is a magazine housed in the pistol. In the police model, the spare magazine bore the figure "2" (even "3" when the weapon was supplied with two reserve magazines).

Another police magazine bottom, marked with a letter "K" in a sun in splendor: probably a marking of the Prussian police

Magazine of a Luger Krieghoff, marked 1937, identifiable by the stamp representing an eagle with a small circle at its center, with the figure "2" inside

Nickel-plated magazine with aluminum base, with "eagle/2" for Luger Krieghoff "S"

Magazine with aluminum bottom with "eagle/63," Mauser production (1936–40)

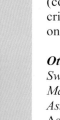

CG 28 / police stamp "Sun/K" on which the figure "3" has been stamped twice. This magazine was to be the third assigned to the P.08 no. 3564. This third magazine was either kept in reserve at the unit or carried by a policeman in a pouch for two reserve magazines.

thick steel, shaped by a press and then machined so that the metal on the body reached a thickness of 0.5 mm. This did not include the lateral braces (corresponding to the position of the line of crimping on the magazines of the previous type), on which the metal kept a thickness of 1.5 mm.

Other models

Swiss magazines for 1906/29 model pistols
Magazines assembled for the French army
Assemblies carried out for the Mauser factories
As has been described earlier in chapter 1, in 1945 and early 1946 the French army had P.08s and magazines assembled on its behalf at Oberndorf from spare parts that were still available at the factory. These magazines differed from the Haenel magazines only in the absence of markings on

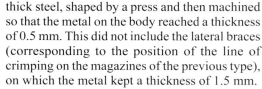

the body, the presence of the only corresponding number of the weapon on the magazine base (without the suffix letter or other stamp), and the fact that the magazine bottom pin is principally blued instead of being in nontreated metal as on German productions.

Postwar commercial magazines.
For a period of several years, magazines very similar to the Swiss model 1906/29, whose single-part body in pressed steel is blued and has a base in black plastic held in place by two pins, had two concentric circles in the style of the naval Luger. These magazines, which sold at a very reasonable price to collectors, offered an excellent operational safety, and Parabellum shooting enthusiasts would have every interest in acquiring one.

This precaution allowed them to keep their original magazines on the shooting stands and to avoid frequent operational incidents with the old Luger magazines.

"Schmeisser Haenel" marking without the initial "H"

Haenel magazine (code "fxo") of a police Luger from the period of the Third Reich. The number "1" indicates that this magazine was normally housed in the pistol.

Haenel magazine (code "122"), with a Nazi police proof mark (eagle / letter "C")

Haenel-made military magazine, with a naval marking

Haenel magazine with plastic bottom (code "fxo")

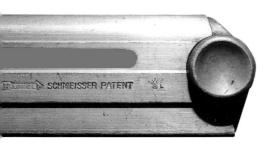

The Parabellum made since 1970 by the Mauser company used similar magazines, but with the base lacking the concentric circles. The rear side of the frame is stamped with the famous logo of the Mauser company. Magazines destined for the Luxury Mauser Parabellum generally received a bottom in the same material (wood, ivory, etc.) as the plates.

Diverse magazines

Along with these large series productions, there were still numerous variants of Luger magazines of Portuguese, Danish, Israeli (marking "codil"), and Dutch, etc. These magazines could come from local production or a reconditioning of the original German model.

Let us remember the existence of particular magazines destined for fire conversions reduced to .22 caliber, and a false magazine in wood called "Füllstuck" ("filler piece"), designed to be inserted in the position of a normal magazine in a wet pistol holster so as to avoid any deformation during the drying process of the holster. A piece of wood with the approximate shape of a P.08 (Holzatrappe) was also used for the same reason.

"Eagle/L" proof stamp of the police, on the body of a milled Haenel magazine

Two variants of markings on nickel-plated Haenel magazine: marking on the right side and marking on the rear face with the initial "H"

Two variants of machining of the top of the reinforcement of nickel-plated Haenel magazines. The one on the right is the earliest variant.

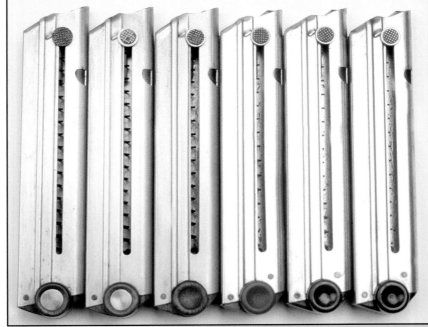

Series of magazines for Swiss Parabellum, *from left to right*: brushed nickel-plated body, thin loading knob, wooden bottom with metal insert; nickel-plated body, thick knob (which was to be kept), wooden bottom with metal insert; nickel-plated body, wooden bottom made by the Berne arsenal (recognizable by the slight flat spot on the fringe of the handling surface). For the Parabellum 00/29: nickel-plated body made in a single part, red-orange plastic bottom held by two pins; Idem, dark-brown bottom; idem, black plastic bottom. *Marc de Fromont*

Reichsführer-SS Heinrich Himmler, head of the SS and the German police forces, firing the P.08

Swiss cross on the bottom of a Swiss magazine for a Parabellum model 00/29

"P" marking (initial of Paillard Ste. Croix) on the rear of a Swiss magazine for Parabellum model 00/29

Red and brown magazine bases of Swiss Luger 1906/29. There are also bases in black plastic material.

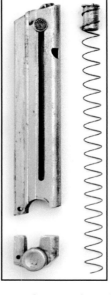
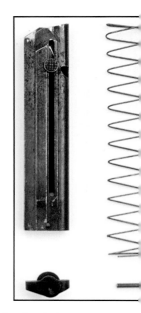

LEFT: A magazine with a body in two parts, with aluminum base, held by a pin at the rear. The spiral spring is topped with a cylindrical aluminum part, which presses against the magazine follower. ON THE RIGHT: a Haenel-type magazine of the type used in service starting in 1938, with a rectangular cross-section spring, a body without indentations on the lower part, and a bottom held by a central pin (here a bottom in black plastic used from 1941).

THE LUGER "SCREWDRIVER"

Military Luger P.08 pistols in service in the German army were accompanied by a spare magazine and a tool used both as a loading tool and to unscrew the screws holding the plates and the firing-pin spring guide. This tool, officially called "screwdriver" by the German army, was housed in a pouch sewn under the flap of the holster.

This type of tool was also made for commercial Lugers and for certain foreign military contracts.

Although this accessory had only minor variations throughout its manufacture, it had a great variety of markings, a sample of which will be presented here.

It should be noted that many screwdrivers stamped with false markings circulate. As long as the marking die had been well researched and well made, the deception is almost impossible to detect. Collectors are well advised, therefore, to be wary of stamped examples.

Single-shot fire devices
Two major types were used to enable the Luger pistol to be used for firing training:

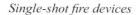

- The most elaborate was made up of a long .22-caliber barrel, a bolt with recoil springs, and a special magazine. These conversions, called "Selbstlade Einstecklauf für Pistole 08" (self-loading insertion barrel for P.08), abbreviated to "SEL 08," permitting repeat fire, were made mostly by the ERMA firm. Their manufacture was relaunched after 1945. The prewar models were presented in two types of wooden boxes,

Illegible markings on a magazine reconditioned by the Portuguese army

Type of marking on magazines assembled for the French army after 1945

Cover of the July 13, 1943, French edition of *Der Adler*, showing a German paratrooper holding a P.08

Base of an East German magazine. The original marking has been removed, then the number of the new weapon was struck.

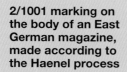

2/1001 marking on the body of an East German magazine, made according to the Haenel process

Strange marking on which an imperial navy–style crown is topped by a letter "N." This "N" is reminiscent of the marking of the North Sea naval base (Nordseestation), which appeared under the Weimar Republic.

"Eagle/6" marking, variant of the inspection stamp for weapons and accessories made by Simson

- Single barrels chambered for 4 mm caliber ammunition with center fire and designed to be inserted in the original barrel. These reducing tubes were fed by hand with a special tool or were used with reduced cartridges housed in the magazine. Due to the weak power of the ammunition used, a manual reloading was necessary between each shot.

- Conversions to one .22-caliber shot used the same principle.

FROM LEFT TO RIGHT: Military tool of the First World War, stamped with a crowned Gothic letter (probably produced by the Erfurt arsenal).
Unmarked tool, probably made by DWM for commercial sale and military contracts. The serial number of the weapon on the back of a police tool. Marking of the imperial German navy (letter "M" topped with an imperial crown).

Mauser military production around 1934

Mauser commercial production, 1935–42

Mauser military production, 1939–41 (Eagle/655)

Mauser commercial production around 1970

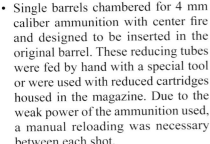

LEFT: French postwar production for the Luger of the French army, (under French control at Oberndorf or made in a French arsenal?). Marking "P.08." The surface against the thumb is checkered.

RIGHT: Portuguese made (period unknown)

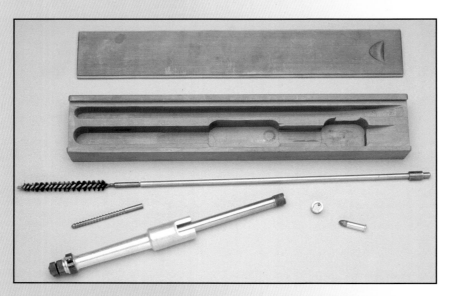

Leinhard conversion, allowing the Luger to be transformed into a single-shot .22-caliber pistol. *Marc de Fromont*

Various 4 mm conversions for Luger with 10 cm and 12 cm barrel in 7.65 mm and 9 mm. *Marc de Fromont*

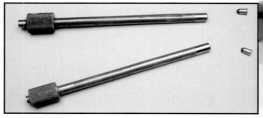

Lothar Walther conversions

P.08 equipped with an "S.E.L. 08"–type ERMA conversion, placed on two conversion boxes: small and large models. As had been designed by the manufacturer, while the conversion was in place the magazine for 9 mm ammunition, the original ejector, and the toggle were stored in the conversion box.

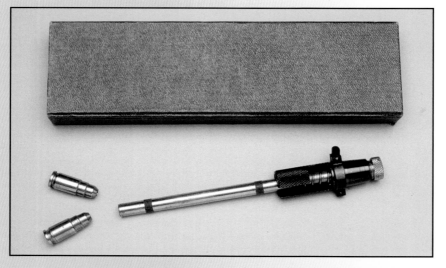

4 mm conversion for Luger in 7.65 mm caliber, with corresponding false cartridges. *Marc de Fromont*

4 mm RWS/Weiss conversion kit. A 4 mm M20 ammunition in the box. The small tool, sometimes called a "spoon," is used to introduce the tiny cartridge in the chamber. After firing, the case is removed, with the rod inserted in the front of the barrel. *Marc de Fromont*

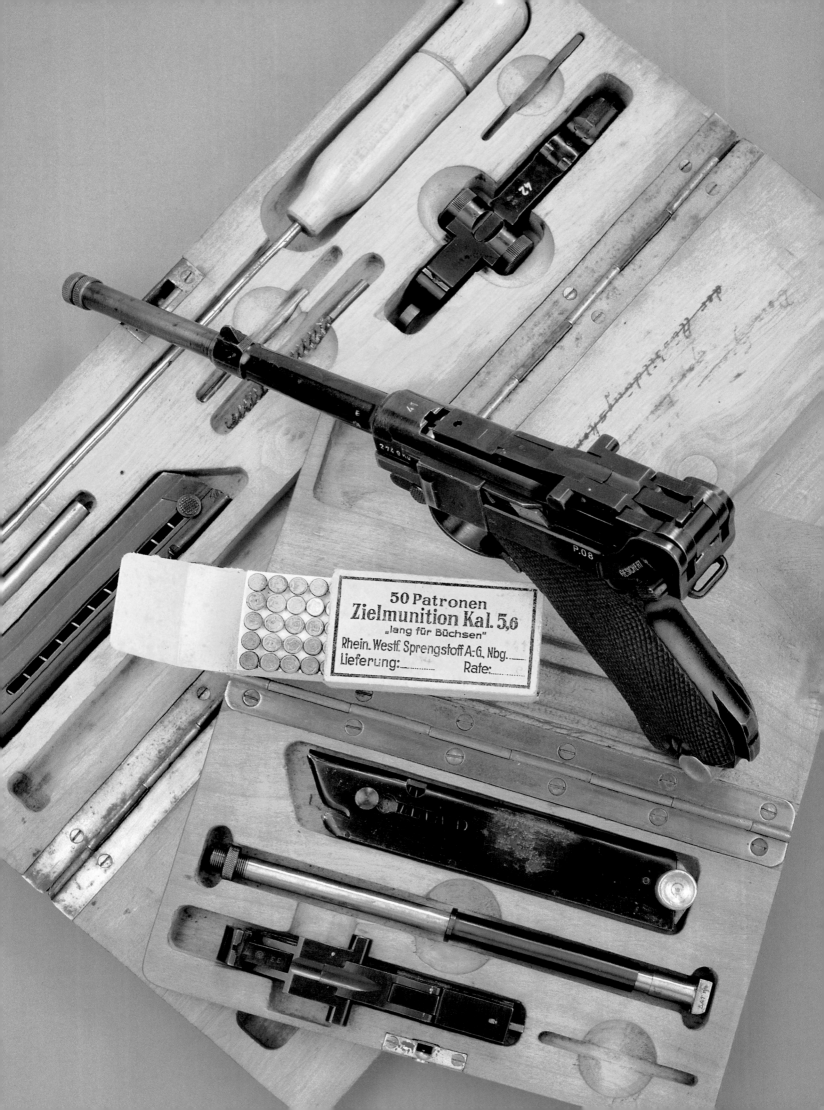

50 Patronen
Zielmunition Kal. 5,6
„lang für Büchsen"
Rhein. Westf. Sprengstoff A.-G. Nbg.
Lieferung: _____ Rate: _____

VARIOUS ACCESSORIES

Muzzle cover in steel made by the Swiss armorers Luthy of Neuchâtel

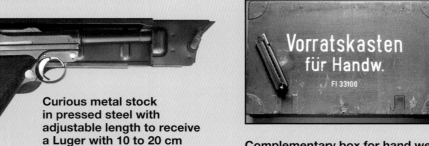

Curious metal stock in pressed steel with adjustable length to receive a Luger with 10 to 20 cm barrel. The origin of this stock remains unknown.

Complementary box for hand weapons (Vorratkasten für Handwaffen). Thi is a box used by armorers to replace parts in the field. Those parts that m often need replacing due to general wear or being lost were placed in tray on two layers. Parts for the 98k carbine can be seen on the first layer and others for P.08 (grips, locking bolts, toggle pin, magazines). These spare parts are generally marked "42" or "S/42." *Georges Machtelinckx*

Tools for drift adjustment of the sights, for Luger 9 mm and 7.65 mm caliber. *Marc de Fromont*

Unlike the majority of Lugers used by other countries, the Swiss Parabellums do not have a lug for fixing the buttstock. These two photos show a test led in this domain by the arsenal of Berne: the grip on the 1900/06 model was fitted with a buttstock to be mounted. The corresponding buttstock is dug from a housing for two spare magazines. *Waffenfabrik Bern*

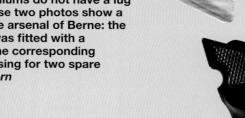

"Arro" grips with thumb support, made after the war in Germany for sports shooters using the Luger

Various cleaning rods, *from left to right*: all-steel model with a small loop, model for Luger with 12 cm and 15 cm barrel with wooden handle, all-brass version (unidentified), steel model with wooden handle for long P.08, commercial version with brass stem and steel handle forming a lubrication tin, and two Finnish models identifiable by their "S.A." stamps (Suomen Armeja)

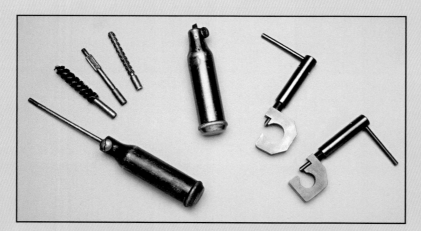

Two takedown and loading tools for Lugers, used as a cleaning rod and screwdriver. *Here*: a version with blued steel body disposed in "cleaning rod" configuration, and a version with a body in brass in transport position, which also corresponds to the use of the tool as a screwdriver. In this position, the cleaning-rod sections, the chamber brush, and the flannelette pull-through are contained in the body of the tool. *Right*: two other types of tool for the adjustment of the sight, one for 9 mm caliber Luger, and the other for 7.65 mm caliber. *Marc de Fromont*

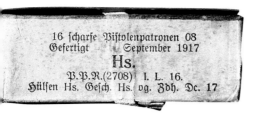

Box for sixteen 9 mm Parabellum cartridges of German military origin (two magazines of eight), made in September 1917

Box of thirty-two cartridges made in Germany under the Weimar Republic. The capacity of the box corresponds to that of the two pistol magazines or a drum magazine for a long Luger or a machine pistol.

German box of fifty cartridges "Oeldicht" (oil tight)

Swiss box of twenty-four cartridges of 7.65 mm Parabellum, made on July 18, 1930

Commercial box of fifty 7.65 mm Parabellum cartridges from the brand "SINOXID"

AMMUNITION BOXES

Old boxes of 7.65 mm and 9 mm Parabellum caliber are not necessarily specific to the Luger pistol. However, collectors of the Luger appreciate having several old boxes in these calibers in their collection. We bring this chapter dedicated to accessories to a close by presenting some of these boxes, the contents of which could have been used in the Luger.

A rare German military box of 1921 and two French boxes: one civilian and the other military

Commercial box of fifty cartridges of 7.65 mm Parabellum, made by the DWM factory in Karlsruhe

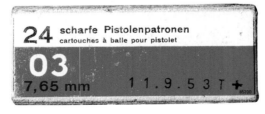

Swiss box of 7.65 mm Parabellum cartridges, made in 1953

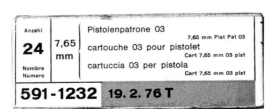

Another type of Swiss box, made in 1976 ("T" for the Thun arsenal)

Box of 9 mm Parabellum cartridges supplied by the national weapons factory at Liege to the Spanish Republicans during the civil war

Two examples of German military boxes of the Second World War, for sixteen cartridges

Box of cartridges for pistol carbine (cartridges with blackened case). These cartridges, more powerful than the 7.65 mm Para for pistol, bear a specific reference number in DWM classification, 471 A, instead of 471 for the pistol cartridges.

CONCLUSION

C reated at the turn of the twentieth century, the Luger pistol holds a particular fascination for weapons collectors today. Even more than the interest generated by its many variants or by its history, it is the visual aesthetic that is at the core of this enthusiasm. The Luger is the product of an epoch where the factories made their weapons with extreme care, and where the inventors associated the need for performance with an aesthetic appeal.

Several Swiss 1900/06s, *from top to bottom*: DWM made with "sun in splendor" motif, no. 8392; DWM-made series E (no. E 756); DWM made with "cross in shield," no. 14543

BIBLIOGRAPHY

Bender, Eugene J. *Luger Holsters and Accessories of the 20th Century*. Dallas: Taylor, 1992.

Datig, Fred A. *The Luger Pistol*. 5th ed. Alhambra, CA: Borden, 1962.

Gibson, Randall. *The Krieghoff Parabellum*. Midland, TX: Gibson, 1980.

Görtz, Joachim. *Die Pistole 08*. 2nd ed. Dietikon, Switzerland: Verlag Stocker Schmid, 2000.

Görtz, Joachim, and John Walter. *The Navy Luger*. Eastbourne, UK: Lyon, 1988.

Henrotin, Gérard. *Le Luger*. H and L Editions, 1999.

Jones, Harry E., ed. *Luger Variations*. 4th ed. Torrance, CA: Harry E. Jones, 1975.

Kenyon, Charles, Jr. *Luger: The Multi-national Pistol*. Moline, IL: Richard Ellis, 1991.

Kenyon, Charles, Jr. *Lugers at Random*. Glenview, IL: Handgun Press, 1969.

Martens, Bas J., and Guus de Vries. *The Dutch Luger*. Alexandria, VA: Ironside International, 1994.

Malherbe, Michel. *La Saga du Luger*. Paris: Crépin-Leblond, 1978.

Reinhart, Christian. *Pistolen und Revolver der Schweiz*. Dietikon, Switzerland: Verlag Stocker Schmid, 1988.

Still, Jan C. *Imperial Lugers*. Marceline, MO: Walsworth, 1991.

Still, Jan C. *Third Reich Lugers*. Marceline, MO: Walsworth, 1988.

Still, Jan C. *Weimar Lugers*. Marceline, MO: Walsworth, 1993.

Walter, John. *The Luger Book*. New York: Sterling, 1991.